Agape

Agape

An insufferably beautiful story of a mother's love.

CLARET SAGE

Copyright © 2024 by CLARET SAGE

All rights reserved. No part of this book may be reproduced in any manner whatsoever without written permission except in the case of brief quotations embodied in critical articles and reviews.

First Printing, 2024

For Sebastian. My Sebastian.
And a commitment to making the decision I can live with if it's wrong.

2003

SHIT

For the first time in years, I feel alive. The way he stands a little too close. His shy laugh at my lame joke. The flutter of my heart when I notice he always detours past my desk on his way to the office kitchen or the stairs to reception. The electricity that courses through me when his hand accidentally brushes mine as we leave the office for our lunch break. My instinctive 'sorry' and his coy but sincere, 'don't be'. We're comfortable. I like it. The way he's interested in me. Genuinely. In me: my thoughts, my dreams, my fears... my feelings. I like it. It's new and I want to soak it up. Ben. I want to soak him up.

The way we hear our own and each other's thoughts in the lyrics of the 90s classics played on the Gold Coast radio station we listen to. The way we can text nothing but song lyrics and feel entirely understood and connected.

The lingering late-night kiss on the cheek that I can't help but lean into. Is that something friends do? I am more comfortable here with Ben, and feel more accepted and respected, than I ever have in my current relationship with *him*.

I've never felt so alive, yet the heavy burden of loyalty looms. Beholden. Trapped. Afraid of expressing my truth. Regardless of how delicately I express it, the response will certainly be irrational and leave me questioning the reality I'm so sure of when I'm away from home. I wish I could escape. Run away and never have to face the conversation, experience the belittlement, or feel the shame. I wish I could dive into the starkly contrasting and welcomed infatuation with someone else. Someone... glorious. Someone predictable, affectionate. Someone safe.

My chest tightens at the thought of voicing how I feel, what I want. Visions of yelling, ridicule, and of course relinquishment. A complete absence of validation. I'm *too* sensitive, *too* privileged. I will, again, assess my own behaviour. Again, find it the cause of the dysfunction. The events of the past two years, how we ended up here, a result of me being too young, too naïve, too determined, too needy, too selfish, too *much*.

One last walk on a lunch break. Painfully beautiful. One last inhalation of what could have been. Poignant. One last haunting kiss on the cheek before letting go. Letting go of it all. The feeling of worthiness. The dream of fun and adventure. Of value. The potential for true love. And for what?

...

Something's off. I can't quite figure it out. I can't explain it or name it. It's just... off. My food doesn't taste right, I can't run fast, I am easily exhausted and quick to feel dizzy. My breasts are swollen and tender. The harrowing realisation of possibility - two blue lines.

The world let out a blood-curdling scream and I swallowed it down. Hard. My future dissolved. A cloak of isolation and loneliness brought with it the deepest inner turmoil. Self-loathing is unchartered territory, but I hate myself. Both for ending up here and for not wanting to be here. A deluge of insufferable guilt and shame.

Disordered thoughts. Chaos. Complete dissociation. This incoherence, lack of reason and unidentifiable emotion is a new state of being. When I finally speak the words out loud, I am met with silence. Days of silence.

It is a decision. But it doesn't feel like a decision. There are options. But they are hidden and secret. And only legal if performed to preserve the life or health of the mother. And regardless of the decision, the judgement is thick.

There's only one decision for me, and that's to give this little human the best of me.

*If you're not surprised with how well they react,
then they're not doing their job as parents.*

Dad is expectedly laissez-faire about it all, Mum anxiety fuelled. I am relieved by their lack of fury. Taken back by their consternation. Grateful for their love, perspective, and ultimate support.

As 'The Little House' slowly becomes a home, my self-loathing morphs to dread. My conscience an oxymoron. Flaky determination. Wavering commitment. Uncertain self-belief. Measured panic. I've got this. I am determined. I am committed. I am measured. And here they are, right by my side. With me every step of the way. My village. He is a mere idle village accessory. At least in my loneliness, I am surrounded by love.

I put aside the dwelling on the immediate and inevitable future compromises and look forward to this new adventure, this new child, and the joyful responsibility. Naturally, I have questions and an exhaustive list of reservations. Conscious incompetence. I'm aware – it's the ultimate challenge. But I'm also aware that not only can I do it, I will do it, and I will do it well. It's going to be one hell of an exhilarating and gruelling ride.

I'm 18 and pregnant. In a disintegrating, obligatory relationship. Riddled with all the things: fear, guilt, shame, and uncertainty. Worry is not something I need assistance with. Second guessing myself is a state of being. I wake in the middle of the night to his head resting on my tummy and I freeze. A flood of intense vulnerability and insecurity. Suddenly and acutely concerned about how I will protect my baby when they're not physically protected by my body. Just one of many situations that should be red flags that I ignore because I'm not capable of addressing them right now. In the months that follow, versions of my circumstances infiltrate the shadows of each eighteenth birthday celebration. Whispers tainted with judgement caress each conversation. Comments breathed with disapproval and pity, void of compassion or understanding. Being pitied is a new and awful experience.

No one says *congratulations*. I see the sadness and disappointment in their eyes even when they don't say it with words. Their grief for what my life could have been. Every. Waking. Moment. Every moment. Is spent fighting my doubts. Reminding myself of the blessing it is to be able to conceive, of how capable I am of raising a child, that I know I will be a brilliant mother. And yet, in these effortful moments of optimism and positivity, one comment, or a misinterpreted glance, is all it takes to plunge me back into the depths of self-loathing.

I'm Richard from *Friends*, each person asking with a sympathetic head tilt, *how you doing? you okay?* And he answers, nodding, *Yeah, I'm okay* with the 'I'm okay head bob.' I despise being looked at as though I am dying a slow and painful death. I staunchly neglect to mention anything negative and embellish all the positives. I am capable. How dare you suggest I am not? I shudder at the thought of how detrimental this could be to someone else in my situation, someone without my strength and support. Someone fighting like I am against the lure of hopelessness. Someone wearing a mask like mine. Someone who one comment might be the difference and add the 'less' to the hope I can see even in the moments I can't feel it. I fear for the outcomes of that someone, and that gives me the discipline to keep my eyes open and locked on hope.

First trimester is shroud in a strange cloak of secrecy, implicit social pity, and a cloud of relentless morning sickness. As an unwelcomed bonus, each month I still get a damn period. It's an actual mind fuck. Teenage pregnancy was never part of the plan. But I got on board. Then I got a period. Confusing to say the least. That resolved, and all was fine. Repeat times three. Yes. Every month. Three months. Honestly. Then high sugar levels. High blood pressure. Potential gestational diabetes and pre-eclampsia. Key word, *potential*. I don't have either. Then warned that the baby is in a posterior position, not ideal apparently. Sometimes I'm sure they forget I'm 18. They forget I've never had a baby. They forget I have absolutely no idea how serious or not serious any of this shit is. They forget, and I continue to learn to embrace uncomfortability – in every sense of the word. Sometimes they can't win. I can't decide if I hate being treated like a child or if I hate it when they don't treat me like one. Typical teenager.

Layla is the most valuable friend to me as I navigate this tempestuous experience. Sometimes, there are feelings and experiences that words can't adequately describe. That's how I feel about Layla. Layla is the perfect balance of compassion and practicality. She understands my fear, she understands my commitment. She understands that sometimes shit just has to get done, and she holds my hand and leads me through it – literally. She leads me to find the medium between stepping up and cutting myself some slack. This is invaluable. But I keep my darkest and most dreaded feelings concealed. The feeling of isolation despite not being alone. The feeling of abandonment because of his abdication. The overwhelm of parenting responsibility that's magnified when cloaked in all the emotions that arise from inequity. My first taste of the weight of parenting with a passenger rather than a partner.

Second trimester has arrived, and the secrecy cloak is lifted. I can share the happy news. Joy. Now it's okay for people to stop whispering their disapproval, and rather, fake approval out loud. I have two major concerns. One, the horrifically uncomfortable transformation my body is enduring, and two, the complete inability to visualise my future.

My tight little athletic body is being abused from the inside out. I'm being stretched in what feels like the most unnatural of ways. My cute little AA breasts are now D cups and creating their own not so little muffin top over my bra. Usually comfortable braless, I now feel my breasts resting on my torso which is especially off-putting. My jealousy for the big breasted beauties of high school has dissipated. My six pack is now more watermelon like, and my skin is itchy. I sleep awkwardly on my side as the familiar position of laying on my front is no longer possible. I look in the mirror and don't recognise the body reflected back at me. I never knew how much of my identity was rooted in my body and what it could do, and I'm grieving the loss of it. Again, conflicted. When considering my body there's both grief and awe.

My future. I cannot see it. Not next month, not next year, not a decade from now. You might think a blank page future screams opportunity. But really, when overwhelming lifelong responsibility casts a shadow over that page, it just screams. Moulding a happy human so they make a positive contribution to the world is simple, right? The thought of owning this responsibility and the selflessness that's required to do so with integrity, is terrifying. Try is not an option. I will. That's no longer the conundrum. It's the grieving of the years I had set aside to be irresponsible, selfish, and egocentric. The realisation that I had assumed this coming-of-age period was a given and naively expected it. The acknowledgement that I am out of phase with my peers. The guilt that washes over me in waves as I mourn what I had pictured for myself before having this blank page future thrust upon me. I can do both. Right? Enjoy my youth and be a responsible capable parent?

Thinking about the future of my afflictive relationship and how to navigate my exit from it is subconsciously silenced by overwhelm and fear, not to mention societal and familial expectation now we are to be parents. The thoughts are never silenced for long. The complete abdication of parenting responsibility yoked with egotistical self-righteousness frequently has them bubbling to the surface.

2004

ISOLATION

All the recounts in the world can't prepare you for labour. You can imagine and empathise. But it's superficial. Like grief. You can't understand until you experience it, and even then, the experience itself is not describable. I have my truth and my lived experience. Others have theirs. This is mine.

Wise or not, this is my excuse to not attend antenatal classes. Fear of judgement is more accurate, but I can't say it aloud. I have read almost everything available. I know the stages, the variations, a range of textbook strategies. I know them as well as anyone can from reading words on a page. Under Mum's coercion, I attend an appointment with an obstetric physio. Less intimidating than a group class. Heather is great. Matter of fact. I like it. Reassuring.

I've almost checked out of preparation. Quite possibly in denial. Or perhaps it's apathy. Could it be contentment? Maybe contempt is more apt. Regardless, it's survival. I can't bring myself to pack a bag, write a birth plan, learn how to navigate hospital carparks and corridors, or exercise discernment when considering attending social events. I regularly remind myself that it won't be like the movies and that I'll have time to do all the things while in the early stages of labour. Going into labour at work wouldn't be the worst thing in the world and it likely beats battling boredom at home, so I'm working to 38 weeks. A subtle driving force is that I've only been with this company 11 months – no maternity leave for me! It's imperative that I earn as much as possible pre-birth.

I have exactly ten days at home before the due date. I've been thinking I might go to 'Ladies Day' at the races tomorrow, 5th June. That's the due date. But what do you know, it's 3am and I'm wondering what that twinge of tightness is. Like a small velvet jewellery bag my inner stomach muscles are threaded with a thick elastic drawstring. It's slowly closed, held tight for a few seconds and released. It was twenty minutes before I felt another, and it was much the same as the first. I couldn't sleep. Too many thoughts, not sure if this is labour. Not sure I want it to be.

I'm still awake at 6am when his alarm sounds for work. It's Saturday. I let him know I'm in labour. He gets up, gets ready for work, and leaves. Perplexed to say the least. But preoccupied with managing myself.

I stay home all morning timing my contractions that ever so slowly become stronger and more frequent, while outrageously inconsistent. I am aware things will get much, much worse. However, in this moment, I can't stop myself from wondering what all the fuss is about. At about lunch time Mum drives me to the hospital and my sister meets us there. That elastic drawstring is being tightened more quickly, is staying tight for longer, and is on a frequent repeat cycle.

I have a lovely midwife. Nurturing. Perfectly balances treating me like an adult but also like a first-time mum. She is easy company. She has me relaxed and trusting her. The hot water of the shower on my back is a relief, and with my sister's help I have the methodical use of the gas down to a fine art. This beautiful woman's shift ends and in comes the midwife from hell. To her I am an object and my thoughts, wants, and questions are irrelevant. I hate her. No understatement. I might go so far as to say she's abusive.

This labour is not exactly straightforward. Baby is not engaged. Contractions are ineffective. The obstetrician breaks my waters, effectively encouraging more efficient contractions. That elastic drawstring is suddenly of extra strength, and I am beginning to see what the fuss is about. Baby - still not engaged. Contractions - still not progressing baby down the birth canal. Decision made for me - injection straight in the thigh to give the contractions some extra oomph. The midwife, at this stage affectionately referred to as Lucifer, interfered with the rhythm of the gas we had established and royally fucked up the one good thing I had going in that room.

CLARET SAGE

I can't do it. As much as I wanted to avoid an epidural, I've exhausted my options and my resolve. I need an epidural and told Lucifer so. For the next 15 minutes she repeatedly leaves and returns, each time double checking, *are you sure?* Yes. I'm sure. Each minute contractions growing stronger, the pressure on my back unbearable.

Lucifer suggests every other possible form of pain relief. Refusing to call the anaesthetist. Continuing with complete disregard for my requests. She leaves and again returns, not having spoken to the doctor. I am filled with unfamiliar feelings of violence. All patience lost and about to lose control, my obstetrician re-enters the room like an angel, or knight in shining armour, or something equally mythical and hope filled. Feeling like a mouse in a lab to Lucifer and biting my tongue, hard, so I don't spit venom at her, I remove myself from the situation and retreat, mentally detach. As I let out a groan to breathe through a contraction, Lucifer forces the mouthpiece of the gas between my teeth. I react, violently slapping her hand away. Seconds later my doctor returns, and his presence alone brings relief. I tell him, plead with him even, to never leave me alone with Lucifer again.

Dad arrives at the hospital having driven him in. Mum and Dad leave me with him and my sister. I am grateful for my sister.

The anaesthetist finally arrives about two hours after my

initial request, and he works fast. Curled in a ball, and after some manipulation, relief. Sensation, but pain free and calm. For a sum total of less than a minute. Chaos hits.

Doctor hits the button on the wall and a loud alarm sounds. Multiple hospital staff arrive and fill the room. Tubes and cords are passed up, over and around. The heartrate monitor is pushed firm into my abdomen, and fluids are forced through the cannula. Zero communication. I have no idea what's happening. I guess there isn't time. My legs are thrown up in stirrups, forceps engaged. Doctor has one foot on the end of the bed, using leverage to free this baby. I feel my vertebrae separating and cracking as I'm lifted from the bed. I wonder how durable a baby is. I hear the doctor suggest baby will be 'in trouble' if they don't hurry. Not realising it was possible, I panic more. I have experience with panic and squashing it down deep inside. I'm accustomed to following instructions in times of high stress. To keep from being pulled from the bed I grip the side bars, tight. I'm terrified. On instruction, I push once, and within minutes of the emergency button being pushed, baby is born, umbilical cord cut by nurses, baby rushed from the delivery suite.

I am in the dark. Is it a boy? Is it a girl? Is it alive? This is nothing like the movies. No screaming slimy baby, no gender announcement, no squirming on my chest, nothing. Just someone stating '4:25pm' and all the people who had frantically run in leave just as quickly. Not a single hospital staff member in the room. Doctor peered from behind the curtain, *I'm still here.* Compassionately fulfilling my request to not leave me alone.

Minutes later, which seemed like an eternity, a baby swaddled in white is delivered into my arms. *It's a boy.* Tears flood my eyes. Happiness or relief the instigator, I can't be sure. Delicate skin, red and bruised. Forceps marks deep in his face. He's perfect.

I am exhausted and so is Sebastian. That's what I named him. Sebastian.

Mum and Dad arrive at the hospital while I'm still in the delivery suite. They wait and walk with me, along with him and my sister, to my room. At 8pm they leave, and I am alone. I have never felt so incredibly alone. Abandoned. Little do I know, this isolation is just the beginning of an enduring experience of solitude. Tonight, I am even without my passenger. I don't know where he is or where he's staying tonight. I don't care.

Night one really is the beginning of the rest of my life. My emotions are fluid and sway between staring at this tiny human in awe and disbelief of what I've just achieved, and overwhelming sadness and despair that I cannot explain or define. The description of such emotion does not exist in the English vocabulary. The opposition of my emotions intensifies and the internal conflict that follows is unbearable. I strangle it. Suffocate it and bury it deep within my soul.

I spend five nights in my private hospital room. I'm young enough to still be considered a child on my parents' private health insurance, I am fully covered. Five nights, completely alone with Sebastian. Despite the queen bed provided, and the father invited to stay, he did not. Not one night. Not even over the weekend. Not a single day off work. Every day was a gruelling challenge masked by strained smiles and cliché responses. The physically painful recovery from the brutal birthing experience, the excruciating loneliness, the floods of distorted reality. I craved emotive empathy but didn't let anyone see it.

Night three brakes me. Sebastian slept well night one, waking for ineffective comfort suckling before falling back to sleep. He too must have been exhausted. Night two was a struggle of very little sleep, relentless infant crying and a hellish battle trying to get Sebastian's tiny little mouth properly attached to increasingly raw nipples and painfully engorged breasts. But night three is unimaginable. Sleep deprivation induced delirium, a duet of incessant crying, bleeding nipples that sting and split further with every attempt to latch and literally growling through gritted teeth to ensure my baby is fed. I call Mum in the depths of the night as I don't know what else to do. I am inconsolable. Unintelligible. Mum understands the gist and delivers frustratingly matter-of-fact responses. *Press the button and call for the midwife. You are okay, and if not, you will be. Put Sebastian down. Have a drink of water. Have you called the midwife? Wait for the midwife.*

All I want is for her to come to me. To come and literally hold me together. Tell me I don't have to do all this. Not even some of it. None of it at all.

She doesn't.

The next few days and even weeks, are much of the same. I force myself to fit the mould and deliver societal expectations, as much as a teenage mother can. Doing the next right thing. Smiling and nodding. Changing nappies. Bathing. Feeding. Delivering the expected responses to the routine questions. Insomnia.

And crying.

Immeasurable, uncontrollable crying. Silent and private tears. Some of awe and happiness, but most of disbelief, despair, and suffocating loneliness. The realisation that I fully comprehend how someone could hurt their own child, and monumental gratitude for Mum whose support is quite possibly what saved me from this awful regret. The fatigue is incomprehensible. Never have I been so depleted of every required personal resource in all my life. My body and my mind ache. I long to be numb, and at times I succeed. Eating and showering is an effort often too great.

I do begin to enjoy motherhood. I can't be sure if this is innate or intentional. But I determine that what I am experiencing - the labour, the difficult people, the various perspectives, responses, and reactions - is all incredibly worthwhile. I recognise that the testing people, the relationships, and the challenging and confronting situations pale in comparison to the miracle of creating a child. Not to mention the privilege it is to have the responsibility of shaping and challenging him to grow into an admirable human, unshackled by convention, empowered to forge his own path in this great world. At this stage, and at each future stage, I learn, over and over again, that I am always capable of the next challenge, despite never knowing what it might be. I will continue to know that neither the good times or the challenges are done, that the loneliness and isolation will not subside, and that I will always know that not only can I do it all, but I will. And I will do it well.

Mum and Dad left for England when Sebastian was just five weeks old. I'm grateful that they were there for those first weeks. They were the most exhausting, emotional, bewildering, and frightening weeks. I did not know exhaustion until I lived these weeks, and thoughts I can't bear to share lingered in my mind. When I feared I had the potential to harm – either myself or Sebastian – I would pick him up, wrapped in multiple blankets, and make the thirty-metre dash in the middle of the cold winter night to the main house where my parents were sleeping. My Mum would take Sebastian and in her calm presence he would settle – and so would I. I would fall asleep on their couch until Mum would wake me to feed him. While I didn't communicate the sobering thoughts out loud, it was a relief that they had resolved by the time Mum and Dad were leaving.

It's a week before Christmas and we've been out for dinner with friends. Sebastian is six months old. Another *family* night out. Another night an entire carton of beer is drunk. Another night I drive home. Another night where incoherence is dribbled, and I work to convince myself it's not worth trying to make sense of nonsense. Remember - do not engage. Another night of carefully navigating the words I speak and the actions I take to avoid an irrational tirade. Another night of music blasting loud into the early hours from the lounge room of our one-bedroom flat while I lay with Sebastian trying to keep him asleep, shielding him from unpredictability, both grateful and regretful that we live on acreage. In a moment of overwhelm, I call Mum in England. She doesn't answer. Is this right? I'm exhausted from trying to figure out what I'm meant to do. Is this what life is? What parenting is? Is this happiness? I work hard to convince myself that I love it all. Because I should. Really, all I know I love is Sebastian. I am trapped by circumstance. Escaping, not an option. The weight of unbearable unspoken expectation is crushing. I can almost feel the walls of the world shrinking, creating a vacuum around me, squeezing the air from my lungs.

My Mum has written back to one of my emails. She signs off with *keep being you and keep being proud of it*. There's so much I'm proud of, but it's shroud in a niggling feeling of fraud. The conflict between what's right and what's easy, self-respect and selfishness. What really is my responsibility? What's the order of priority? Where does meeting societal expectation sit in this order?

2005

LOST AND FOUND

This is my year. It's for me. I'm going back to uni. I'm ready to show the haters they are wrong, that my life is not over, and I most definitely will amount to something. I continue to learn, however, that there will be a long list of compromises and endless obstacles to navigate. Mum and Dad are back from England and just knowing they are here is comforting. Sebastian is enrolled in a family daycare. As the household income consists of an apprentice wage and whatever part-time income I can get, a significant proportion of daycare fees is subsidised – what a relief. Sebastian is enrolled three days a week. And I have managed to find a course of study that I think I'll enjoy and that allows me to be at home twice a week. I do my best to enrol in most of my classes over those three days. I will have to work to catch up on the classes I miss on the days I can't make it.

I am enjoying new people, building new relationships, doing something on my own and for me. I'm enjoying the interest people have in me. No one knows anything about me unless I tell them. Then they only know what I tell them. I love this. I get to decide who I am, and quickly, I'm realising I'm not sure who that is.

I can easily list the things I like to do: touch football, netball, writing, sketching, music. I love going out and dancing to old-school rock cover bands. Beyond what I like to do, who am I? So much of who I am has become being a mother. And again, there's the conflict. The guilt born from not being okay with motherhood defining me.

Rebekah is in all my classes and I've come to learn our childhoods were spent in the same community. We know of each other's families without knowing each other. Rebekah is my security blanket outside of home. I trust her. I trust her to be judgment-free and honest. Very quickly I am more honest and more vulnerable with her than I have been with anyone. She knows me. She knows how I feel about my life better than I do. She knows I feel trapped at home and free at uni, and somehow gives me the confidence to give myself permission to not only figure out who I want to be but to make it happen.

As Rebekah and I drive to our lectures together we sing loudly to Panic at the Disco. The regularly dysfunctional air conditioning means we have the windows down, hair whipping our faces for the short stints we're not sitting in traffic. When we're not singing, we talk. Bek is a brilliant sounding board never hesitating to give it to me straight.

I learn early on that if I want time away from Sebastian and I want to be able to relax that I need to arrange a babysitter. I begin learning this when my first attempt at time away from Sebastian lasts only a couple of hours. I have left him with his father. After being at the venue less than an hour I receive a call instructing me to come home. Sebastian won't settle. Sebastian is being driven around the front paddock. Driving on the road isn't an option when you've had as many beers as he has. There is so much wrong with this story. Rebekah highlights each concerning facet.

Spending a night away from home one weekend I leave Sebastian with Mum for the night despite his father being at home at the very same property. Sebastian being with Mum allows me to relax and enjoy myself. I planned to stay at a friend's house and return home in the morning, however, plans change and I decide to return home to sleep in my own bed. I arrive home and after checking on Sebastian in the main house, go to climb into bed in my little flat out the back. I'm surprised to find the bed empty. I'm curious. It's midnight. Where is he? He said he'd be at home. I make a phone call and ask where he is. The answer I receive is "at home". To avoid backlash I question very carefully and receive the same answer. This time with venom. How dare I be so accusatory. I reply, measured but with emphasis, "*I* am at home. *You* are not". And hang up the phone. At some point the next day he arrives home. There is no mention of where he'd been, no discussion about the reason for the deceit. On the outside it is as though nothing happened. On the inside my thoughts are disordered and clouded by questions of my ability to reason.

Rebekah is perplexed and directly lets me know – this is not okay.

Rebekah is 18. She's carefree but her morals are clear. Some of the experiences I share with her I don't share with anyone. And she is concerned. There are other stories, incidental anecdotes, that I don't share. If I don't say them out loud, I can try to pretend they didn't happen. The casual lying about having quit smoking, what our money has been spent on, or why he's home so late. The punched walls during arguments. The aggressive insults. The reckless driving in response to noticing a speed camera flash. The walking out and driving away to avoid uncomfortable conversations. The instructing me to leave the room to breastfeed. The excessive drinking accompanied by blaring music into the early hours of the morning if we've had an argument. And if we haven't. The perpetual lack of consideration or contribution.

Slowly but surely, all of the not okay things of the past that have been shroud in denial are coming into focus. Gradually and deliberately, I am beginning to question and to communicate what I need. Mum's words, *keep being you and keep being proud of it,* circle my mind. How do I be a me that I'm proud of?

I had fallen asleep putting Sebastian down for a nap one

CLARET SAGE

Saturday afternoon and am woken by a knock at the door. It's Mum. The look on her face is concerning. She's not okay. She tells me there's been an accident. A car accident. My aunty has been killed. My aunty who holds a particularly special place in my heart. My godmother. My home away from home. Mother to my closest cousins. My legs give way beneath me as I struggle to believe what I am hearing. My thoughts are unintelligible -- my mind and body both failing me.

Quickly I realise that my experience does not compare to that of my uncle and my cousins. Tragically, my aunty was not the only person killed in this accident. Her mother was also killed. My cousins had lost their mother and their grandmother in the blink of an eye, one ordinary afternoon. Others lost a sister and a mother, another lost a wife and a mother-in-law, and another lost a wife and a daughter. I need to pull myself together and be a support, in whatever way I can for my family who are experiencing indescribable grief and pain. I'll start by simply being there.

I have experiences of death. I have buried countless pets and animals. I have lost a grandparent, and I have friends who have grieved the deaths of their parents. I am learning though that I do not even begin to comprehend it. How do you define existence? I do not cope when things don't make sense. I very much need my wonderings to have answers. I have been able to accept death in the past. But this. This is simply absurd, senseless. I can't understand it, and therefore can't accept it. Strangely it's two Einstein quotes that help.

He said that there is not matter, just energy. And that what we have called matter is simply energy whose vibration has been lowered so we can detect it with our senses. He also taught us that energy cannot be created nor destroyed, rather it can only be changed from one form to another. This allows me to understand that she has not ceased to exist. Rather, her energy has changed and is no longer detectable by my senses. She was not destroyed, merely transformed, and continues to exist. This gives me enough peace to begin to work towards acceptance. I am hopeful that one day I will be okay with not knowing, and never understanding why.

2006

HEARTBREAK AND HAPPINESS

As Sebastian gets older, life is getting a little easier. He's approaching two now. We are still regularly plagued by sickness – pneumonia, asthma, various allergic reactions – and sleeping through the night is not even close to consistent. But we are nappy and bottle-free. This slightly lightened weight of parenting responsibility has further increased my awareness of my lack of satisfaction. Along with continuing to enjoy uni life – the relationships, the freedom, the learning, the general broadening of horizons – it's highlighted how unsatisfied I am with my life at home. At home I feel like a slave to the solitary confinement of sole responsibility.

On two separate occasions, I have tried to communicate this. Delicate, intentional planning of how and when to strategically approach the conversation where I voice my experience, share my perspective. I shared that I'm not content, tried to express what I need. Each time met with hostility and belligerence, followed by a swift exit and days of absence. Not only reluctance but brazen rejection of the necessity to communicate. Even to simply listen. There has been literal headbutting of a car resulting in a busted nose, baseless accusations of infidelity, questioning of my perception, and blatant refusal to seek understanding. I am regularly told I don't make sense, labelled as overreacting, denied any memory of my attempts to communicate my discontent in the past, and told that I must stop letting my family get inside my head – that damn silver spoon I've had in my mouth since birth is tainting my perception of what I deserve.

The weeks between attempts to voice my wants and needs began with token gestures of service. However, the lack of shared responsibility remains. The lack of any attempt to understand, or listen, or make real change, remains. These months have been stressful. A constant state of tension. I don't know why I can't share this with anyone. Perhaps shame. Definitely fear. Of what I'm not exactly sure. This I will not share with Layla, or Rebekah, or my parents. This I suffer alone, without conscious reason.

It is a relief to push it from my mind when I am with my uni friends. I am spending more nights out with them, and I am lapping up every ounce of attention that comes my way. I continue to learn that not only do I want more, but I deserve more. I am learning I am desirable, and others are willing to give me so much that is more, and better. The possibilities are exhilarating, and I relish flirting with my own boundaries. Especially in the days where he'd left.

I regularly question how to be proud of myself and how important perception is – that of my friends, parents, family, and the rest of the world. I'm not sure why I don't communicate with those closest to me. I don't think I can bring myself to acknowledge what's coming. I'm petrified. Of so many things. I am in a constant state of uncertainty. Standing, blindfolded on a cliff top. Toes curled over the edge, wind tousling my hair. No comprehension of what it will look or feel like when I take the plunge, completely uncertain if it's the right thing to do. Right for Sebastian. Right for me. But I am growing confidence, every day, that it is what's necessary.

The other day I received an unexpected email from Layla. She feels excluded and hurt as I'd been to lunch with some friends without her. My capacity to manage another relationship right now is non-existent. I wish I could find the empathy for how she must be feeling, but I can't. I'm utterly exhausted and consumed with coming to terms with the demise of the normal I have come to know. Her email was hurtful and accusatory. I felt attacked. I was angry. I replied. I don't feel good about it. The back and forth was quite respectful considering how hurt we both were. The words I wrote: *I am so completely over having to explain myself and the way I want to live my life to people who quite obviously aren't worth it* - I know the words aren't for Layla. She made comments like, *I am over people stabbing me in the back the first moment they get and if I don't stick up for myself no one else will. I am tired of trying to maintain friendships with people that put me down every chance they get.* I wonder, are her words really for me? I briefly consider what Layla must be dealing with in her own life that she's not shared with me, or that I don't understand, or maybe that I haven't listened to, but the thought is brief. I just don't have the capacity to take that thought any further. We apologised, expressed that we understood the other was hurt, and that there aren't any hard feelings. But we also both expressed that we didn't have the energy required to save what really was the most beautiful friendship.

It's heartbreaking.

Layla. The first person to know I was pregnant. The person who drove me to the doctor. The person who told me I'd be a great parent and showed me the silver lining. The one who had the presence of mind to think practically and helped me to put one foot in front of the other when I simply did not know what to do and may have hidden in bed indefinitely had it not been for her love. She's the one who treated Sebastian like family, the one who was free of judgement and who not only accepted but supported the way I balanced raising an infant while trying to enjoy my teenage years. I don't have her anymore.

It's a significant sacrifice for someone I'm growing to hate.

I remind myself, again, that all of this is not for him. It's for me. It's for Sebastian. It's because I know that my choices are mine and I need to be able to look back and be happy with the way I handled myself.

For the third time I speak the words. This time less considered. *I'm not happy. I need to talk to you about this.* He begins to stand and my heart pounds. I cannot let him avoid this again. I cannot watch him lose control, disappear for a few days, and return full of empty promises and superficial gestures. All the while refusing to listen to me. Refusing to hear my feelings and my needs. I say, quiet but clear: *If you go without having this conversation do not come back.*

He left.

Each time he left, he did so without discussion. He did so without a thought for Sebastian. Not so much as a goodbye. This time was the same. Only this time, he left for weeks.

The past few weeks are a blur of relief, grief, and self-discovery. I've danced with strangers, reconnected with friends, fielded horribly uncomfortable questions and frustrating proclamations of the appropriateness of my decisions, said yes to almost every invitation, relied heavily on my parents for babysitting, and slept with anyone who made me feel heard and valued. It was both agonising and glorious. Most importantly, it was necessary and liberating.

It was during this time that I began to build a relationship with Arlo. Why Arlo? In the beginning, it was because he, like the others, made me feel wanted and desirable. But he is different. More than. He listens. Deeply listens. He genuinely cares. He is confident in himself. Considered. There is no desperation, I am not filling a need. Being with me is a choice, a want. He chooses me, and he allows me to choose him. He's independent, expects me to be so, and loves that I am. He is spontaneous but not impulsive. Full of surprises but never reactive. He thinks I'm worth fighting for, and he's one hell of a fun time. And he is constantly surprised by how easily I am impressed by him. I am slowly learning that this is what I deserve, and it's a completely reasonable expectation.

I'm sure navigating the demise of a long-term relationship is tricky for anyone. However, at 21, navigating the demise of an almost 5-year relationship that involved not only joint assets and finances but also a two-year-old requires significant strategy and composure. Compound this with a complete misalignment of values, and I am learning very quickly about the nuances of people management. While there is relief that I will no longer flinch with the slammed doors and the punched walls, what I was not prepared for was the mental exhaustion of attempting to co-parent with an emotional abuser. I will have to continue to manage someone who thrives on telling me what I think rather than asking, saying something happened when it didn't, or stating something wasn't said when it was. And there's the acknowledgement that Sebastian will likely continue to endure it all. A debilitating acceptance.

CLARET SAGE

Staying calm and measured above all else is gruelling. When I am lied to or patronised, I am calm. When he wakes me with a call at 1:00am and informs me that he's at the airport with Sebastian boarding a plane to Brazil, and that I will not see my boy again, I stay calm. This composure, consideration, and commitment to clear, exact, and unmistakable communication is something I will come to master.

I have two years of my degree left and I am becoming impatient. I have been living my life on someone else's terms, captive to the subtle criticism and blame that has allowed a sheathe of self-doubt and questioning to form over the years. I hadn't noticed my usually assured self crumble. It's time to seize the potential, the opportunity that lies ahead of me, and no longer be a passenger in this life of mine.

2007-2011

ABRIDGEMENT

I accelerate my study to take six subjects a semester and subsequently graduate early, allowing me six months to explore my new career before guiding Sebastian through his first year of school. My decision has me disconnect from my uni peers somewhat as I am out of sync with them, but I have a renewed sense of purpose and drive. And thankfully, I don't disconnect from Rebekah.

I explore Sebastian's Michael Jackson infatuation, his obsessions with G.I. Joe figurines and the Wiggles' Big Red Car. I am privileged to watch and learn as his cheeky and charismatic personality emerge and am in awe of his natural aptitude for dancing and his physicality in general. He is a conversationalist, a natural social entertainer. These years are a hive of activity with Arlo and me buying a block of land and building a house, getting engaged and then married, and committing to further study: Arlo a career changing bachelor's, and me a master's degree. After a heartbreaking miscarriage, we fall pregnant again, and while life is naturally permeated with challenge, I am living the life I want. One full of love.

The raising of Sebastian is not what I would describe as a co-parenting situation, unless I was referring to Arlo rather than his father. Adjacent parenting may be more appropriate, which, however, is still a more favourable description than the reality. The chain is lighter, but still connected to the shackle. Without question I have this complex and exhausting situation to thank for my refined relationship management skills and my invaluable nuanced communication. The forethought, the strategy, the remarkable composure. The development of the thickest of skins. The persistence and the tolerance, and the finding of the appropriate lines between uncompromising and submissive, empathetic and dissociative. Whatever the most appropriate adjective for the dynamic, it is indeed relentlessly arduous.

In many ways Alannah is my saving grace through these years. In the beginning, Alannah was the new girlfriend, but she has quickly become my piece of mind whenever Sebastian is at their house. Alannah is my closest thing to reassurance that Sebastian will be okay when I am not around. Not too long after she joins Sebastian's life, I decide to call her. We have quite an open, possibly confronting conversation. While I am utterly dumbfounded as to how this is who she has fallen in love with, selfishly, I am grateful. Not surprisingly, it is significantly more important to me that Sebastian is okay than that Alannah is making good life decisions about her romantic relationships. During the phone call I explain to Alannah my parenting philosophy, I am upfront about my reservations when Sebastian is away from me and the quality of care he is being provided, and that I need her to assume the mother role in my absence. I make it clear that in my opinion she is the best parent he has when I can't be around, and that I need her to fill that role. While I do want her to consider me, my approach to parenting and what I want for Sebastian, I do not want her to be second guessing decisions or holding back on what she thinks is right in terms of responsible parenting for fear of stepping on my toes. There's no doubt in my mind that Alannah is my only hope of any form of genuine, loving, proactive and responsible parenting happening in that house, where I can't be. Alannah is grateful for the call, relieved even. And it is the beginning of what will grow to be complete mutual respect that will last long after the demise of their relationship.

2012

PULL OF THE TIDES

Michael is born in February. Sebastian turns eight in the June. This new experience of parenting stands in firm opposition to what came before. Parenting alongside Arlo is a partnership founded in trust, respect, and open, honest communication. In addition, I am self-assured, calm and confident. Decision making and problem solving are not things we do to or for each other, they are things we do together. Raising Michael with the existing step/co-parenting of Sebastian has resulted in a significantly more complex family and parenting dynamic.

Sebastian's emotions are unexpected. The assumption that love is limited and therefore a portion of my love had to be taken from him for me to love Michael. The subsequent re-assurance and careful explanation that a mother's love grows. There was a surprising definition of 'real'. Sebastian determined that Arlo's love for Michael was *real* because he was Arlo's *real* son. Even more challenging was the speculation that Michael was a child born from and into love, and that Sebastian was not. The insight of a seven-year-old is staggering. The impact of these wonderings on Sebastian and his wellbeing is significant and I'm not prepared for it. Another parenting challenge that results in me feeling alone in navigating the nurturing of Sebastian. This time through his feelings of worthlessness. Being worth less than, rather than worth nothing.

I am wrapped up in love and support and empathy by countless people. I am not alone in this journey. But the isolating feeling of being alone in my responsibility, perceived or otherwise, is heavy. The unrelenting consideration for the impact of my life choices on others - Sebastian, Arlo, Michael - is a weight I'm not sure how to carry, but also unsure how to let go of. The reluctance to share the weight of this onus for fear of adding to the burden of others is a vice in my chest. There's constant consideration and questioning of my responses, my methods, my decisions, even the most minute. These are only the beginning of the significant emotional challenges Sebastian is to face, and therefore just the beginning of my journey of loving him through them.

The parenting challenges that rise from life organically are complex enough. This year I'm learning that the most challenging experiences are the ones that are imposed upon me by those I respect the least. The challenges I face because the choice of who influences my child is not mine alone.

CLARET SAGE

This year Sebastian is playing soccer. He's loving it and shows impressive goal-keeping potential. Occasionally, all four parenting figures are on the sidelines. While I struggle through these moments, I'm happy for Sebastian. Mostly. It's May. I am holding three month old Michael while Arlo and I watch Sebastian warming up on the field. I see he and Alannah walk towards us. He has a broken leg. He broke it in a recent car accident. The small talk doesn't extend beyond this. The lack of detail is intriguing, but I don't ask questions as great conversation has the potential to result in conflict.

Weeks later I receive a call. He is calling to tell me that Alannah has left him, that he has lost his license, and that the accident resulting in his broken leg was a single car accident. He drove into a tree while almost four times the legal blood alcohol limit. Another epic display of reserved, calm, and considered communication. There are two very triggering things he says in this conversation. He repeatedly tells me this isn't fair because he 'did the right thing'. After a night out drinking, he caught a taxi home in the early hours of the morning. He awoke a few hours later around six to head to a game of golf. He wrapped Alannah's car around a tree on the way. My attempt to voice that this is not 'the right thing' is fruitless. He's seeking my empathy and friendship, stating that with Alannah's exit he feels like he's 'living his life over'. I am direct in letting him know I am not the person to seek empathy from, and that perhaps, now might be the time to learn. There is no acknowledgement that this was the result of him not taking responsibility for himself or this ultimate act of selfishness.

Swallowing my contempt, hard, I ask how he planned on transporting Sebastian without a license and without Alannah. The lack of sound planning led to change in care arrangements and in 2012 at eight years old, Sebastian came to only visit his father every second weekend. This was my silver lining.

Anxiety creeps back in knowing Alannah is absent. There is a new female housemate, Kate. Not romantically involved, who I have some faith in. Sebastian is in no way her responsibility and she seems to be sure of this; however, in moments of need she always delivers, and I am very grateful. Sebastian comes home with stories of not being well and Kate taking him to the chemist, or in the evenings when his dad is partying, Kate feeds him dinner and plays with him in the mornings while his dad lies 'sleeping' on the couch.

This is the first of many challenges these few years will throw at us. I am enjoying my study and have returned to full time work to allow us to manage financially. Arlo is well and truly into his degree and has moved to balancing full time care of Michael as well as continuing with his degree. In addition, Arlo is battling severe sciatica that continues to increase with intensity despite rehabilitation efforts. Surgery is necessary and to manage this unexpected expense we are renting out our family home and moving back into my childhood home with my parents: me and Arlo, Sebastian and Michael.

Multi-generational living has been a growing trend for a while, but it wasn't one I was hoping to contribute to after moving out only three years earlier. Ultimately, it's a positive experience. My parents are some of the most generous people I know, and willingly give not only their home, but their unwavering support through time, effort, and love. The feeling of imposition is unavoidable and one I do not enjoy.

It's a challenge for Arlo as he is 'home' all day, in a place that is not his home. He is the home keeper – school drop off and pick up for Sebastian, primary carer for baby Michael, as well as a full-time study load – in a place where he feels not at all at home. No amount of generosity or support from my parents can change that. It is also proving a tough year for Sebastian. An only child for eight years, now sharing all things with a brother. The shift in care arrangements without a clear understanding of why. A child, living in a house with four adults, leaves no room for tiny misdemeanours to go unnoticed. The pressure of feeling under a microscope, the confusion surrounding a father who can't drive because of 'a broken leg' that's taking years to 'heal', the uncertainty of whether a mother's love can grow... it's tough. There is a lot of anger. Frequent teary meltdowns, and less frequent but significant fits of rage accompanied by an inability to identify why. Subsequently, we went to a series of visits to a most wonderful psychologist. If I could bottle what this man gives

Sebastian, people across the world would be at peace. It is not a cure, it is not 'the answer', but it is a relief. I can see it in his face and his little body each time we leave his rooms.

Living back at the homestead, as a family of four, was a necessary challenge. Arlo finishes his degree at the end of 2013 and secures his first teaching job at a school just a few minutes from our family home which we moved back into in October. It has taken a couple of months to settle back in, and we are now delighted to be pregnant again with another baby due in August. 2014 is set to be a big year, with Arlo working full time in his new career, and another baby on the way. But this is just the beginning.

2014

BEGINNING OF THE END

I learn through text message, with one week's notice, that his work arrangements are changing. He'll be working a 2/2 swing roster in the mines. I'm told he'll tell Sebastian when he collects him from school and takes him to soccer training. After a year and a half, he can drive again – that leg is finally healed. There are no replies to my texts seeking clarification. I am careful not to ask specific questions.

I am told. Not asked. It is not a discussion. There's no mention of change to care arrangements. There is zero consideration for anyone other than himself. No consideration of me, which I have come to expect. But absolutely no consideration of Sebastian. None. No comprehension of the fact that this decision has an impact on other people. I am careful with how I seek clarity. I seesaw in and out of the illusion of control. I have lived the experience of him twisting my words before holding them against me. Of him making irrational decisions because I've somehow implicitly planted the seed of

AGAPE

a foolish idea. Considering explicitly asking what his plan is for care arrangements has the heat of fear rise from my chest and grip my throat. What if his response is a suggestion I can't bear to contemplate? The not knowing, the unpredictability, the irrationality. It's both easier and safer to assume he will continue not considering Sebastian. The thought of two straight weeks of not having to consider him, of not having to worry, of not needing to consider all possible responses to any set of circumstances, to ensure I'm armed with the best response to keep my son both physically and psychologically safe, is a most alluring thought. You can imagine then, the opposing emotional state, when I consider the possibility of Sebastian being away from me and subjected to the relentless volatility for a two-week period without respite.

Sebastian is dropped home after training and the car drives away. A single wave of acknowledgement through the window at most. There are no pleasantries exchanged between he and I. Sebastian walks in through the front door and I quickly learn that care arrangements are changing from one long weekend a fortnight in his father's care, to an alternating two-week schedule. Because that's how custody arrangements are made, by using the ten-year-old as a messaging service. I briefly explain to Sebastian that while this might be what his father has told him, and it might be his request, it is not in fact a decision or an agreement.

The adult discussion of the proposed change to custody arrangements never occurs, and this is just the surface of the string of inappropriate incidents and empty and irresponsible promises over the next few years.

I'll be there to watch your soccer game and take you home with me for the weekend from there.

He doesn't arrive at soccer and does not communicate that he's not coming. In the evening of the same day, he sends a text, twenty minutes before arriving at our house, informing me he will collect Sebastian.

I'll see you in a fortnight!

Irregular and unpredictable changes to his working schedule, no proactive communication, often resulting in Sebastian not seeing his father for over a month.

Can't wait to spend the weekend with you!

Only to ship Sebastian off to a babysitter on his return from weeks working away so he can spend time with his girlfriend, and explicitly sharing this with Sebastian.

In planning to take Sebastian to America for his brother's wedding, I say I will sign the passport application if he agrees to provide me with a detailed itinerary, update me regularly of any changes to said itinerary, and ensure I always have accurate contact details. Despite not a single aspect of this agreement being met, Sebastian goes on the trip. I am indebted to his sister for providing anytime access to communicate with Sebastian and a thorough itinerary. During the two-week trip, I receive regular distressed phone calls from Sebastian from his Vegas hotel bathroom because his father and new girlfriend are experiencing the nightlife. Sebastian is left at home with the grandparents – repeatedly. The shattered heart of a mother who sobs as she listens to her child's abandoned tones, literally from the other side of the world, is the worst feeling of powerlessness.

The unpredictability, lack of reliability, and constant disappointment continues on the return home from America. Car trouble the enduring theme.

I'll drop your America souvenirs to your house on Monday. Doesn't happen. Car trouble.

We're informed via email from the soccer club that 'Sebastian's Dad' will now be the team's coach. *I'll bring the souvenirs to training on Tuesday.* He doesn't arrive at training. The players are left stranded. There's no delivery of souvenirs. Car trouble.

I'll bring the souvenirs to training on Thursday.

He doesn't arrive at training. Players (and parents), stranded again. Still no souvenirs. Car trouble.

You can imagine the response when the other parents

wonder why Arlo isn't conducting the training sessions. For the first time ever, I make it abundantly clear that Arlo is not Sebastian's father. Furthermore, that we do not associate with him, nor do we have any idea what is going on in terms of coaching and reliability – we are as perplexed and frustrated as the other families.

The impact on Sebastian is significant and accumulative. Intense anger. Tears. Yelling that he wants to scream and punch things as he clenches his shaking fists and exclaims that he is sick of broken promises. When we arrive home from training this Thursday evening a box of souvenirs rests at the front door.

Car trouble continues to be the reason for absence or lateness to training and competition games. I wonder if 'car trouble' includes not being able to start your car because the law-enforced interlock system won't allow it? In a period of eighteen months, Sebastian spent a total of ten weekends with his father. I never say he can't go. Likewise, I never say he can't stay with me. Routinely, I arrive to collect Sebastian from the house he stays in when with his father (his grandmother's house), and he has not seen his father in days. These weekends are included in the ten.

Regularly, I am informed of Sebastian witnessing fights between his father and the girlfriend involving screaming profanities and throwing things at each other. One time they fought at a party, and both left the premises, forgetting that

Sebastian was there. Not dissimilar to the time Sebastian was dropped home after school and left alone while his father went to play a round of golf, not to return until after dark. He's nine. This emotional dismissal is compounded by the pointed conversations Sebastian is subjected to, instructing him to put in more effort so the girlfriend feels included.

Repeatedly, I listen to Sebastian attempt to rationalise why the girlfriend is his father's priority. Empathise when he tells me he doesn't want to spend time with his father anymore and watch the disappointment on his face when I inform him that his father's "not sure" when this swing will end and when he'll be able to see Sebastian next.

Sebastian not spending time with his father suits me. But it crushes Sebastian. The peaks and troughs of false hope and rejection tear him apart, one fibre at a time. I struggle not to unravel with him. The frustration of the lack of financial support, and a complete absence of any understanding of shared parenting responsibility, lingers in the shadows of my mind. Half of the school fees are paid directly to the school. Every other associated cost of parenting rests with me and Arlo. Uniforms, books, stationery; doctors' visits and antibiotics; the general costs of day-to-day living; every significant and insignificant thing. It was the disparity, not the dollars, that bothered me. The prevailing disparity, from pre-conception to infinity, that I am simply unable to accept. This flippant opt-in opt-out parenting style oozes rights and abdicates responsibility. It leaves my soul to bleed. There was even a trip to

Mexico without so much as mentioning it to me or Sebastian. Literally MIA and uncontactable for weeks.

Mid-year, amongst the chaos, our third son is born. Jimmy. A welcome surprise for this year is also the rekindling of my relationship with Layla. A beautiful full circle moment of mutual respect and forgiveness, and a genuine love and commitment to rebuilding the beautiful friendship that we walked away from almost ten years ago.

This year is the first time Sebastian asks to see his father when he is meant to be at my house. I could tell he was off. He had been up and down all day. Angry. But not open to talking about it. In a rare demonstration of empathy (or perhaps spite), his father picked him up and had Sebastian for the evening. The conversation, however, was littered with comments of Sebastian being a spoilt brat who gets whatever he wants. My response was that I didn't see it that way and that I hoped, should the situation be reversed, that Sebastian would be able to ask me about spending some unscheduled time with me. It is only weeks later that I find myself incredibly grateful for the way I handled this situation.

December is the first time Sebastian explicitly asks not to go to his father's. He has asked in the past, but as the day approaches, he changes his mind. This time is different. As the day draws nearer, he becames more adamant. Sebastian says he wants to wake up with our family and his brothers on Christmas morning, see his father for the middle of the day, and return to where all the kids are for the evening. When I communicate this with his father, he refuses to have Sebastian in the middle of the day if he's not staying for the evening, claiming the only reason Sebastian wants to spend time with his father and extended family at all, is to cash in on presents. I empathise and explain that we as parents make the decisions, but we must listen to Sebastian, and then communicate our decision. The response to Sebastian from his father is, *if you don't want to be here, I don't want you here. I'll see you next year.* Then he ended the call.

2015

GAMES

You fucking hurt my feelings.

You and your mum need to stop playing stupid games and get your shit together.

Don't bullshit me, Sebastian!

So, what, I'm not your family now?

Your mum just sits on her arse at home and has kids so she can be on endless holidays.

You cannot talk to your mum about anything that happens in this house. Ever.

Wow. Welcome to 2015. This is the string of abuse that Sebastian copped on the way home to his father's on New Year's Eve. Sebastian relives it as he gives a theatrical recount a few days later. He thinks he's depressed - but only at his dad's. While he's there he just doesn't want to get out of bed. *What's the point, I'm only going to be ignored or yelled at.*

Am I living some sick parody of Roald Dahl's Matilda that's missed the satire? I take a risk. I'm not sure if it's a good one or not, but I tell him all the negative things he tells me about his dad's house make me not want to send him there. *I don't blame you,* he says.

My heart. Shattered and bleeding for my child and the life he has to endure. A life I created and am responsible for. A life so far from the ideal that I had imagined for any child I would bring into this world and nurture. The familiar emotional conflict of heartbreaking empathy for Sebastian, and the overwhelming shame of not being able to save him from this battle permeates my being.

Hi. My name is Sebastian. I'm here to tell you why I want to be school captain and let you know the qualities I have that would make me a great choice.

I want to be school captain because I want to give back to this wonderful school for the quality education and endless opportunities it has provided to me. I am grateful for what this place has given me, and I want to make sure that all the students in the future continue to be provided with these things. Some of the opportunities I have most enjoyed are being involved in the musical, talent quests, inter-school sport, and the futsal carnivals.

I have many qualities that would help me to be a great school captain. I am caring and compassionate. I am committed and am willing to give up my time and to be available for short notice jobs when teachers or kids are in need. I am confident which allows me to speak well to large groups and be a good representative for our school. I am approachable and willing to listen, so if you have any questions or requests, I am happy to listen and do what I can to help. I love working with other people in groups, but I am not afraid to work alone if necessary.

I want to be school captain and today I have told you why I think I would make a good one. Whether I am voted in or not,

I will be a senior student who is a great role model to my peers and a great representative of our school.

Thank you.

Sebastian is unwell and therefore can't attend school today. It's the day speeches are being delivered – so he will miss out. However, reading Sebastian's words and discussing with him his desire to be a positive influence in his community, has me flooded with comforting pride. A strange emotion to connect with pride but raising Sebastian has been unsettling and I have spent much of the journey learning to rest in discomfort. Hearing his vision for himself and acknowledging what he has to offer is indeed a comfort and reassurance that we are heading in the right direction. 2015 will be a good year.

As always, despite prior agreement, I send a confirmation text on Friday afternoon after a paediatric appointment, letting him know I was on my way to drop Sebastian off. It seems I will never learn to expect unreliability and am shocked when I hear back that this can't happen. He's gone out. I can't expect him to wait around forever. Don't I know it's a Friday night? He said he'd collect Sebastian on Saturday instead.

Sebastian is more upset than usual and asks to call his dad to ask why. When they speak, the only reason provided is *I'm in the city*. Sebastian ends the call and cries uncontrollably, heaving tears. *Why does Dad keep doing this to me?* Via text I let his father know that Sebastian is not okay. The only response is that he seemed fine on the phone and that he's sure one more night won't hurt. Sebastian does not want to go to his dad's tomorrow. In his words, he feels rejected. He pleads with me to go the following weekend instead.

The subsequent phone conversation:

> Me: *Sebastian is feeling really rejected and doesn't want to come to your place this weekend. He'd prefer to come next weekend.*
>
> Father: *That's not happening. I'll pick him up in the morning.*
>
> Me: *I need you to know he's really quite upset, and adamant that he won't be coming.*
>
> Father: *Let me talk to him on the phone.*
> *(enables speaker phone, passes the phone to Sebastian)*
>
> Sebastian: *Hello.*
>
> Father: *You better know what this decision means. Do you realise what you're doing here? If you choose not to see me tomorrow, you won't be seeing me next weekend. I'm busy. Is that what you want?*
>
> Sebastian: *Yes.*

CLARET SAGE

> *(call disconnects)*

Sebastian completely breaks down. Again. Staccato breaths break up the distressed phrases.

> *What's wrong with me?*
> *What have I done wrong?*
> *Why is he punishing me?*

Supporting a child through such emotional abuse is heart wrenching. A confronting challenge when you can't help feeling that you're enabling it but have no idea how to prevent it. The thought of taking preventative or protective action is laced with the fear of enabling or encouraging something more damaging.

I scrutinise every decision. Those past and those yet to be made. I know, above all else, I need to be there for Sebastian, to hold him together, physically and emotionally, as I watch him dissolve under the weight of his father's words. Despite Arlo and I having planned a weekend away to celebrate a family wedding, with prior arrangement to leave Michael and Jimmy at home with a sitter, we take Sebastian with us to our booked accommodation and forfeit our attendance at the wedding. I cannot leave Sebastian. He is feeling abandoned and rejected and punished by one parent already. I need to give him all of me.

I can see in these moments the array of emotions churning in Arlo. As usual, he gives me what I need, including complete understanding and empathy. I can only imagine the anger at play, and the frustrating experience of this unfolding around him. I know I'm not alone in the intense feelings of isolation. I'm sure Arlo feels it too. I try to find the capacity to be empathetic to him, or at least acknowledge the challenge. I'm not sure I succeed.

Despite years of never claiming child support and not engaging lawyers, the time has come to seek genuine advice. I am out of resources – emotional, physical, and cognitive reasoning. I make an appointment. I have equal parts hope and fear.

Subsequent communication with his father is hostile.

If Sebastian wants to see his dad before I go away again, he can give me call. I'll be away for his birthday.

Sebastian is not interested in giving him a call.

I take it you didn't tell Sebastian about my text and seeing him for his birthday, or has he decided he doesn't want to see me. Which one is it?

I tell him Sebastian wants to wait and see how he feels after his birthday.

Why, because he's too busy?

I explain that Sebastian is too hurt and angry, not too busy.

So, he is angry at me because I didn't come and get him last Friday night, yeah? Or is there more to it and I should call and ask him myself?

I explain that Sebastian does not want to talk to him.

I'm at the point where I'm trying to make decisions that are the least damaging. I feel completely helpless and incapable of making decisions that will have a positive impact. There is a complete lack of clarity and confidence. All thoughts of how to navigate this situation, of what's best and what's right, are hazy. Like driving on the freeway in the dark of night during heavy rainfall. I can't see the lines on the road, the light scatters and splinters as the raindrops fall, signs are illegible, and I don't know which exit is mine. It's unnerving, disorienting, and disempowering.

The appointment with the lawyer is intense and frustrating. As opposed to intensely frustrating. While my expectations for my child and how he is treated by a parent may be at a particular standard, the system has a starkly different understanding of what's acceptable. I am advised that if I go through mediation or even family court, the resulting shared care arrangement would be less favourable than the current situation. It is recommended that I pursue child support and encourage his father to see a counsellor. Neither of these things is going to happen.

Agreeing to see a counsellor would require some level of self-awareness and willingness to learn and evolve. The response to me suggesting such a thing would be volatile defensiveness as I would certainly be coming from an assumed superior position. My anxiety associated with the possible ramifications of pursuing child support; the potential to motivate him to seek additional time with Sebastian in his care soley to avoid payment of support, is terrifying. The wellbeing of my child does not come with a price tag.

There is a fundamental lack of empathy, an unbearable arrogance, and inflated sense of importance, coupled with highly irrational responses to benign situations let alone occasions of some significance. Equipped with knowledge gained from experience, fear pervades any thoughts of the future and my ability to navigate it in a way that ensures Sebastian's safety and a loving childhood. I am trapped and suffocating in this life I don't feel I chose; in a relationship, I'd murder if I could. The times I have wished he would just go, cease to exist, or dematerialise, are too many to count and a stark reminder of just how exhausting having to consider him is.

A birthday card has been hand delivered, labelled *Sebastian*. It is from his father. $50 is enclosed with a benign message. Sebastian is non-responsive to my suggestion of sending a thank you text or making a phone call. His father eventually calls and asks to speak to Sebastian.

I can hear the yelling as I stand beside Sebastian, but I can't make out the words. Sebastian becomes very upset, is not saying a lot other than 'no', and eventually hands me the phone. It is my turn to cop the hostility.

> *You don't know anything about discipline.*
>
> *Sebastian doesn't want to see me because he gets everything he wants at your house.*
>
> *You should be making him call me on special occasions, not just letting him get his own way all the time.*
>
> *That Friday night I did nothing wrong, why the fuck would I just wait around for you to drop Sebastian off after an appointment – it was a fucking Friday night!*
>
> *I don't even have a relationship with my own son.*

I draw a long deep breath in and blow out my hatred and detest, slow and steady. I remind myself of my why.

> *Do you want one?* I ask.

Silence.

I tell him I am happy to meet with him to sort things out and following that, bring Sebastian to meet with him, as long as I determine it to be a safe, unthreatening environment. He doesn't understand the concept.

He says he wants Sebastian there so we can catch him out on his lies and games and so he can't play us against each other. I explain that's not the reason to meet, and his tirade reignites. I end the conversation.

Sebastian is angry. The angriest I have ever seen him. Violent tears. Kicking and screaming as he sobs in his bed. Yelling at me that he never wants to see his dad again, that his dad is trying to turn him against me, that I need to go to court because something needs to be sorted out. The most heartbreaking part is the profuse apologising for making everyone's lives hard. If it wasn't for him the rest of us would not have to put up with his father.

All I can do is reassure. I muster all my courage to continually withhold my own opinion of his father. I shower Sebastian in all the specific things I love about him, reassure him that he is a blessing and remind him how grateful I am to have him in my life. Tell him that we love him, that we need him, that we enjoy having him around, and nothing can change that. He really struggles to fall asleep tonight. As do I.

Sebastian's birthday comes and goes. There is a short surface-level phone conversation between Sebastian and his father that ends without conflict. Over the weekend, whenever anyone doesn't live up to expectations – they are late, don't cook what they said they would for dinner, don't put their cup in the dishwasher – Sebastian says, 'they did a dad. Get it?' We talk about that not being particularly respectful, but he simply responds with a shrug of the shoulders saying, 'It's true. And it's funny'. He's 11. This is his way of accepting his father the way he is rather than expecting him to change. I'm not sure whether this makes me proud or sad. Maybe both.

In the following weeks, Sebastian decides he would like to spend the weekend with his father. When we speak about the change of heart, Sebastian simply says that this is his dad, and he wants to see him even if he is the way he is. We discuss various strategies of how to not escalate situations, and how to cope if yelling, swearing, and blaming begins, and some simple safety planning should things escalate.

The next couple of months, and the two weekends that he spends with his father, are largely uneventful. While this is a relief, the hypocrisy is jolting. I'm sending my child into an environment that I don't think is adequate, one that has the potential to be damaging. He'll be in the care of a biological parent, so therefore it's acceptable? It's not. It physically hurts. I don't feel like I have a choice but to endure the pain. A hand has ploughed through my sternum, curled its fingers methodically around my heart and squeezed. An unrelenting vice. This feeling, these inadequate control measures, engaging in the activity regardless – this is not something I had predicted would be part of my parenting journey. I certainly didn't predict safety planning would be part of my children spending time with a parent.

While there were a couple of good months, it's not long before I am subject to another tirade about my substandard parenting. It begins with a relatively benign logistical conversation about transport. While Sebastian was in his father's care, I went to watch him play a soccer game. His father left the soccer game without communicating with me or Sebastian. I called him when the game was over as I didn't want to leave Sebastian at the venue alone. He gave me the address of where he was – a birthday party. Suddenly, I am being lectured. I am completely blind-sided. He begins attempting to educate me about Sebastian's behaviour. That it is unacceptable. That it's my fault. That I need to pull him into line. That he's always disrespectful. That this is somehow my fault despite him being the parent who has left his child at a public venue while responsible for him.

I again draw that familiar deep breath. This time, for the first time, I use my out breath to calmly let him know that child management, educating young people, teaching them appropriate behaviours - this is what I do. It's what I am an expert in. It is what I have done, and have studied specifically, for almost the last decade. I explain that there are clear expectations at my house and appropriate, logical consequences – reward and reteaching. He tells me that he has told Sebastian his behaviour is so terrible that it's making him not want to spend time with him.

Another deep breath. I choose not to speak for fear of spitting venom.

Dear Sebastian,

What an amazing milestone for you – you're finished primary school! How far you've come from that skinny little ragamuffin who used to cling to me and cry each morning as I dropped you off to school. How you have grown and what you have learnt over the last seven years is nothing short of phenomenal. Arlo and I are incredibly proud of the person you are today. You are a person of courage, strength, love, compassion, and determination. The quality of yours that most impresses me though, and that makes me most proud, is your moral compass. Your ability to know what is right and what is wrong and how you're not afraid to stand up for injustice is inspiring. It is this quality that will no doubt lead you on the path to success and happiness.

You are the most amazing big brother to both Michael and Jimmy. Arlo and I know that being the older brother of two boys who are much younger than you are, and who at times test your patience, is not always an easy role to play. When you play with them, teach them, and show them the ways of the world, I am constantly reminded of how lucky they are to have you and how they will grow to be better people because they had you as their brother.

CLARET SAGE

Sometimes I know that it's difficult to look at the world and think that it's a wonderful place. Things can be difficult; especially when you're young. However, if you continue to view life and the world as an opportunity for learning, you can't go wrong. Learn more about yourself, learn more about your family and friends, learn more about the people who annoy you most, learn more about the tiny little things and the big things in life. With learning comes understanding, and with understanding comes peace and happiness.

If I have one wish for you going into high school, and even beyond that, it is to be happy with who you are. What is success? Some people find that a difficult question to answer, but for me it's easy. Success is happiness. I wish that you are always happy with who you are, what you have, and what you do. On top of that I hope that you never question just how much I love you and how incredibly proud of you I am.

You're growing up so fast,
And I wish I could make each moment last.
My little boy will someday be a man,
and right by your side I will forever stand.
I will pick up the pieces when you fall,
and hold your hand to help you stand tall.
And when the day comes for you to go on your own,
never feel that you're all alone.
No matter how near or far apart
I am always right there in your heart.

Always remember:
Whatever you go through,
No matter what,
I will always love you,
Not a little – a lot!

Love always,

Mum.

Dear Sebastian,

Congratulations on graduating from primary school!

Your Mum and I are so very proud of you for this achievement and for the young man that you are growing into. You have come a long way in the last seven years. I can only imagine what you will accomplish in the next seven years of your life.

Some of your best qualities are your compassion and your optimism. You always watch out for others, and you are extremely considerate. You never let anything get you down for too long and you are quick to see the positive side of a bad situation. These are some of the best qualities that people can have, and it makes family life with you so much more enjoyable.

You are an extremely intelligent and determined young man. I can't wait to see what the next chapter of your life has in store for you. Most importantly, I am looking forward to seeing how you deal with it.

Always remember that your Mum and I will always be with you and always love you. No matter how hard things seem, if you use your strengths that I mentioned above and remember that your family will always be there for you, there is nothing that you cannot overcome or achieve.

Love Arlo.

Graduation letter from his father:

2016

THERE IT IS

After years of carefully navigating all the lines - uncompromising and submissive; empathetic, dissociative, authoritative; rights and responsibilities. After years of questioning the importance of parental presence, even if significantly less than ideal, questioning what's ultimately damaging and ultimately positive, this is the year I grow to know exactly where my line is. And commit to scoring it so deep that it scars.

The beginning of the year is unexpectedly eventful. Sebastian embarks on his high school journey and learning a significantly more complex environment. Navigating new buildings, new friendships. The public transport system is overwhelming at times, but he handles it like an absolute champ. Sebastian's greatest strength is his social game, and his greatest challenge is organisation and attention – an interesting recipe for a boy entering adolescence. These events are expected. An unexpected event is the premature birth of our fourth son, Thomas, in the first week of school. I know it's going to be a big year with Sebastian starting high school while we have a new baby. In addition, I have taken a full year's leave to not only be more present for the boys but also to lay the foundations for a small business of my own. I know I'm in for a big year, but the monumental challenges I am yet to have thrust upon me are simmering undetected below the surface ready to detonate.

Two weeks into the school year I learn, through Sebastian, that his father is no longer working away. Anxiety mounts. I fear a request to return to the equal custody arrangements of four years before. This fear is physical. I feel ill. Constantly. I can't bear the thought of Sebastian having to endure the experience of his father any more frequently than he currently does. There has been a steady decrease in the amount of time Sebastian spends with his father over the past four years. It began with the DUI and loss of license leading to a decrease from fifty-fifty shared care to one weekend a fortnight, and subsequently further decreased by the fly-in fly-out arrangement resulting in visits with his father occurring less frequently than once a month.

When I muster the courage I ask for a conversation about care arrangements, and he says he will call when he's free. He doesn't. He doesn't see Sebastian for the first month he's not working away. A pattern begins to emerge where he intermittently and unpredictably asks if Sebastian can stay at his house for a few days. Sebastian always wants to come home on Sunday and begin the school week at our house, and so he does. In addition, Sebastian often declines the invitation to his father's if it coincides with a school event like camp, a swimming carnival, or a talent quest. He prefers to leave for those events from our house. On this occasion, Sebastian chooses to go to his dad's on Friday afternoon, and this time agrees that he will stay three nights, and return home after school on Monday.

Sebastian arrives home – on Sunday. This is unexpected and the only communication includes a text message received twenty minutes before they arrive. He's angry and confused. His two-night stay had not been enjoyable. Sebastian tells me that on the way home from school on Friday afternoon he was berated by his father for many things, including only spending one night with his father during this visit. This was confusing for him as he had chosen to spend three nights, however, his father had arranged for him to spend the Saturday night with a friend, and despite Sebastian saying he would stay the Sunday evening, his father dropped him home to me. Sebastian describes the verbal assault on Friday afternoon as full of screaming and swearing as they drove, for decisions that were out of his control. He describes the rest of the weekend as tense. He was afraid to do anything for fear of being attacked for decisions that weren't his. Once again, Sebastian doesn't want to go to his father's and is highly concerned things will become more volatile if he does.

Again, the very fibres of my being are under tension. Pulled in opposing directions. Not able to define what the ethical and morally sound decision is literally hurts. What is right? I'm analysing my motivations for considering each possible response. The overthinking. Questioning what's driving me. Fear? If so, is this justifiable? Is it Sebastian's best interests? Am I sure I even know what they are? Where is the reliable research on best outcomes for children in his situation?

Easter is approaching. Sebastian is torn. He tells me he doesn't want to go until the school term is over, that he doesn't want to be there for very long, and that he wants to start the next school term from our house. I let his dad know via text, after my phone call went unanswered, that he can pick Sebastian up from school on Thursday, the final day of the term, and I would then pick him up on Easter Monday.

I receive no response, agreement, or acknowledgment.

It's the night before he is due to collect Sebastian from school. I still haven't heard anything. Anxiety mounts. I'm not sure why or about what. I think it's the thought of sending my child to be in the care of someone who is so unpredictable. Unreliable. Someone who I feel I have very little control or say over whether or not Sebastian should be allowed in his care. Any other adult I felt this way about, Sebastian would never be allowed in their care. How can I be confident Sebastian will be nurtured, looked after, loved? How can I be confident I'll be able to contact him and communicate if he can't engage in a discussion of simple details? Again, I seek clarity about whether Sebastian should catch the bus home to our house or if he will collect Sebastian from school. The reply is stilted and lets me know he will pick Sebastian up on Thursday afternoon, but that I need to collect Sebastian on Saturday or not until the following Wednesday, as they are going away. Sebastian calls his father to ask questions about where they were going and who with. He answers the phone, but the conversation is brief and vague. The answer to where - "away". The answer to who with - "friends". Sebastian tells his father he would rather come home on Saturday and hands the phone to me. The call had ended. I confirm in a follow-up text that he will collect Sebastian from school on Thursday, and I will pick him up on Saturday. I do not receive a reply.

Sebastian left for school on Thursday morning not knowing how he would get home, and to which house he would go, as the confirmation communication had not been reassuring. Sebastian and I decided that if he didn't hear from his father throughout the day, he was to catch the bus home, and keep me updated every step of the way. At 4:30pm Sebastian let me know he had done well in cross country that day, and that he had been collected from school by his father.

As a parent, I believe in trusting your intuition. But I also believe in being reasonable and considered. There are times when this creates significant personal conflict, and sending Sebastian to his father's this weekend was one of those times.

2016

MY FUCKING LINE

Good Friday

5:20pm (Text)
What are your plans for tomorrow? I am more than happy to pick Sebastian up at a time that suits you. Otherwise, let me know what time you'll drop him home.

7:30pm (Call) No answer. Message left.

7:45pm (Call) This time Sebastian's phone. Off.

8:00pm (Call) No answer. Message left.

8:45pm (Text)
Could you please let me know what is happening tomorrow so I can sort out my day?

9:15pm (Call) No answer. Message left.

I'm worried. I'm annoyed I didn't trust my intuition. I'm working hard at maintaining perspective.

I have not had communication from his father in the past week. The only communication was a text from Sebastian that he had been collected from school.

9:45pm (Text)
Help me. Dad's drunk. I'm scared.

Fear courses through my veins and I don't know what to do. Before I can think, another text.

9:46pm (Text)
Come to the unit. Now.

I immediately call. Sebastian answers. He's whispering, but hysterical. I can barely make out his words through the tears. He says he's scared. He repeatedly tells me to hurry up. To hurry up and save him. Save him from his dad.

> *Who the fuck are you talking to?!* Screamed with violent intent from the background.

The phone cuts out. Moments later, my phone rings. It's Sebastian. He is still hysterical. Still desperately pleading with me to save him. Still not giving any detail. The self-control you can exercise when your child's safety – physical and psychological – depends on it is remarkable. My voice, calm. My breath, steady. I stay logical. I de-escalate Sebastian. He's able to provide detail.

> He tells me he is in his cupboard.
> He tells me this is safer than being outside,
> but scarier as he can't run if his dad opens the door.
> He tells me the girlfriend is there.
> He tells me he can't tell if she's drunk or not.
> He tells me his dad is going to kill him.

> I tell him I need to hang up so that I can call the police.
> I tell him to call the police not me if anything changes.
> I tell him I will be there as soon as I can
> and that I will do everything I can to keep him safe.
> I tell him I am proud of him.
> I tell him I love him.
> I tell him again.
> I tell him one last time.

I hang up. One of the most difficult things I have ever done. The thought, whether rational or not, that you may have just told your child that you love them for the last time, is one harrowing thought. A thought that I quickly box and shove down into the depths of my subconscious.

I am with my sister and her husband, as well as Arlo and our three little boys. My sister and I get in the car and go to the apartment. It's a 40-minute drive. My sister drives, I call the police.

10:00pm (Text)
All good. In bed.

This is not Sebastian. They have taken his phone. My imagination explodes and fear invades my veins. I am powerless. Helpless. It's a most horrible feeling.

We arrive at the unit complex. I do not know the unit number. We wait.

And wait.
And wait.
And wait.

An agonising wait.

There isn't a word for the emotion I feel when the police arrive at 2am. I am asked a string of questions. What type of person is he? How should we expect him to respond? Has he been in trouble with the police before? Then they go up to the unit. They are gone all of five minutes before returning to me in the carpark.

'He's a piece of work, isn't he?' Followed by comments of his obnoxiousness, the fact that he was clearly intoxicated, and unreasonably demanding of them. They tell me Sebastian is asleep and that the girlfriend has been sleeping in the room with him. They say he's safe, but they're not sure whether he would be if the girlfriend wasn't there. While speaking with the police, he calls my phone, and the police instruct me to answer. I answer and put him on speaker. He's angry.

> *Why the fuck are there two policemen at my door?*
>
> *Sebastian was scared.* Calm. Measured.
>
> *Why THE FUCK are there two policemen at my door?* He's irate.
>
> *To check on Sebastian.* Effortful composure.

He spat venom at me through the phone. Screaming, swearing. Telling me Sebastian is fine and that I can talk to him to prove it.

> *Can he come home?* Quiet fear.
>
> *Yeah, he can fucking come home, if you fucking come get him.* He spits.
>
> *Let me talk to him.* Careful hope.
>
> *Please come and get me. Please take me home. Please Mum.* Sebastian was... Not like Sebastian. Quiet tears. Whispered gasps.

I tell his father I am coming to take him home, and he hangs up. The police say they will come up to the room with me but stay out of sight. I walk to the keypad; the police tell me the room number. The intercom connects but no one speaks to me. Screams from the speaker echo through the car park.

> *Get the fuck out.*
> *Get down the front.*
> *Your fucking mother's here.*
> *You're never seeing me again.*
> *You're never coming back here.*
> *Ever.*
> *You can fuck right off.*

The police inform me that the lift stopped on level two and is now returning to the lobby. Sebastian and the girlfriend walk out of the lift and towards me at the door. Sebastian launches into my arms and I envelop him. Tears stream down his face as he clutches me and whispers,

> *What took you so long?* His wet eyes holding mine.
> And my heart.

In this moment there's a fleeting sense of gratitude for the girlfriend. As she walks away, I look up and say thank you. She turns on her heel, pierces my eyes with hers, and through gritted teeth she hisses,

> *He's never seeing any of us ever again. Not us, not his grandparents, no one. His father's really upset.* Then disappears into the lift.

Does she think that's a threat?

I comfort and reassure Sebastian, wrapping him up in my arms and my love, telling him how proud of him I am. I can't tell how much of this is for him, and how much of it is for me. When he's in my arms, I know he's safe. I want him in my car, doors locked, protected, as soon as possible. I get that done and speak with the police about my best course of action. They tell me to keep Sebastian in my care and make it very clear that I am not legally obliged to allow his father to see him. They recommend I seek legal advice as a matter of urgency. My phone rings. It's him again. The police advise me not to answer. They tell me they will wait until I have Sebastian settled in the car and am ready to leave before they go. Soon after, both he and his girlfriend arrive in the car park. The police officers keep them away from me and my car. Eventually, they return to their apartment. I sit in the back seat with Sebastian while my sister drives us home.

It's a quiet drive. Sebastian has very little to say, but what he does say is harrowing.

> *I thought I was going to die.*

I've been scared before, but I've never actually thought I was going to die.

Dad threatened to kill me.

Why did you take so long? Why did you take so long to save me?

Dad kept throwing things at me. His phone and his watch both hit me.

On Saturday afternoon Sebastian asks if he can tell me what happened. He speaks, I listen. That's all. His words and expression – dissociative.

During the day Dad got really angry at me for choosing not to spend Easter there. He said 'Suck shit, you're not coming on our holiday. Heaps of people will be there. Everyone is really angry that you're not coming and you're going to hear about it.'

In the afternoon we went to the neighbours. Me and their daughter went to see a movie and get some ice cream. When we got back, she said, 'Your dad is so drunk.' I didn't want to look at him. When I did, he couldn't walk properly. The ladies had left and gone to bed. Because Dad couldn't walk properly and was mumbling, the neighbour walked us back to our unit. Dad kept knocking on other people's doors. Being stupid. When we got into the unit I went to bed.

Dad walked to my room and mumbled to me. I couldn't understand what he was saying. Suddenly, he pegged his watch at the wall and walked out of my room. I went to look out my door and Dad was right there. He started yelling, screaming, 'Yeah, I'm still here mate' and slammed the door in my face.

I could hear him throwing things and slamming doors. Yelling at her too. Lots of swearing at her. It sounded like he was throwing things at her. I got scared and called you. He came in, ripped my phone out of my hands, and threw it at me. It hit me. He left again, slamming the door and yelling, 'I'm going to kill you'.

She came into my room to calm me down. Dad barged her out of the way, yelling 'You're a lying cunt' at me at the top of his lungs. She went and tried to calm him down, and again he started yelling at her. He said that if she didn't get out of his way, he was going to throw her out of his way. Later she came back into my room and sat with me for ages. I must have fallen asleep.

I woke up to Dad yelling at me calling me a cunt and a fuck wit. 'You're a fuck wit, why are the police here you cunt?' He said it over and over. Then he called you and you said you'd come and get me. Then you buzzed and he got so angry that you got there so quickly. He started yelling that he was going to go and punch Arlo's face in. Then she said she'd walk me down.

I called 000 twice but Dad kept walking in, and I would hang up before he took the phone.

I was yelling, 'Help' at the top of my lungs. No one came to help me.

I thought I was going to die.

I thought about running out of my room, out of the unit, and downstairs. But there was so much banging I didn't know if I'd make it. Then I wished my room had a lock so I could at least lock myself in.

The experience of this night, and that of the days that follow, is surreal. On one hand, there's significant mental haze. On the other, crystal clarity. Validation and confirmation in the most unwanted way. My phone conversation with Mum while sitting in the car out the front of the unit waiting for police thrust me into internal childlike distress. There are offers from friends and family of both practical and emotional support, both appropriate and inappropriate. The legitimate offer of bikie intervention was more tempting than I'd like to admit. The realisation of the level of negative emotion I could harness towards a person and the harm I could wish upon them was confronting and overwhelming. I didn't know I had the capacity to hate.

I contact the lawyer who I have consulted once before. He outlines two options.

Option 1. Don't do anything.

If his father gets in contact, explain that Sebastian is still traumatised from the events of the evening of Good Friday, and that he will not be seeing Sebastian unless it is in a public place, supervised by someone I know, who has the independence to call me if he becomes a danger to Sebastian.

The positive of this option is that Sebastian stays in my care, and that I avoid all costs. The negative of this option is that if his father gains access to Sebastian, he can take him and leave, and nothing can be done about it. I could request a welfare check, but ultimately, unless the police believe Sebastian is in imminent danger, they will not remove him from his father's care.

Option 2. Begin court proceedings.

Apply to get a Certificate from a Dispute Resolution Practitioner to start court proceedings. I could possibly get an exemption since there is evidence of family violence or abuse – but only if I have substantiated evidence. In the case of Friday night, there is the risk that a judge doesn't think this is severe enough to warrant exemption from an attempted mediation. Therefore, before wasting money on court proceedings based on an exemption and risking the judge sending me to mediation anyway, I must invite his father to a dispute resolution with a mediator. A private mediator is the best suggestion for a significantly more favourable outcome. However, considering the circumstances, the likely outcome of mediation is that his father will have regular unsupervised access.

The direct advice? Write a statement that outlines all communication and events from the week prior, including a running commentary of the conversation with Sebastian where he recounted the events of Friday and Friday night. Send this to the lawyer. Then wait.

Should his father express that he wants contact, and is persistent, contact the recommended mediator and begin the process of requesting his father's attendance at mediation. Contact the lawyer when I am aware of the response to the request – either that he will attend or a certificate has been issued because he has refused to attend or respond.

I am grateful that these next couple of weeks are school holidays. There are multiple episodes of significant emotional distress. Sometimes, usually in the evening, Sebastian begins to sweat. He turns red, starts crying, shaking, and rocking. He violently wrings his hands, and on the bad nights, he bites himself. Hard. There are times it is the opposite. He is empty. Vacant. Non-responsive. Sometimes triggered by feeling unsafe at bedtime, scared that his father is in the cupboard, or startled when he shuts his eyes and sees his dad screaming at him. He's petrified that the court will force him to see his dad. Sebastian's reality is that his dad tried to kill him.

He's petrified, and I am petrified. And lost. I have no idea what his dad's intent was. But his impact was significant trauma. And not only on Sebastian. Watching him fall apart piece by piece, not being sure of the boundaries of his emotions and mine, is disorienting. There are two things I'm sure of, and only two things: my hatred and my insufficient resources. Relying on hope to combat uncertainty becomes tiresome when uncertainty prevails. My mind does some interesting things. Sometimes, I'm not sure what's reality and what's imagined. Like when listening to the tick-tocking of a clock. Despite the sounds being identical, we attribute different sounds to the tick and the tock. It's interesting how the late Frank Kermode describes the different sounds, 'Tick is a humble genesis; tock the feeble apocalypse'. This waiting is the most interesting experience of time and I fear the feeble apocalypses will be as perennial as the tock.

Uncertain. Hopeful. Humble. Feeble. At a minimum, am I adequately keeping up appearances? The last thing Sebastian needs is to be worried about his mother. I need him to know that it's okay to have lost all resources, even if I'm finding it hard to believe it myself. How do I ensure he knows he can rely on me when I'm failing at holding it together?

'Do you know what it's like to hate your own Dad?' 'Do you know what it's like to know that you're part of someone you hate?' The regular probing prelude to the meltdowns. Perhaps an expression of isolation. Empathy deprivation. I don't know how to separate my experience from his to adequately support him through it. The weekly psychologist appointments, for both Sebastian and I, are beneficial and necessary. But progress is slow.

INFINITE

ANDI

Andi. A nickname only I use to name my anxiety. Andi has been around for as long as I can remember. They existed for a long time without a name. It was in these years that their influence over me, control even, was significantly greater. In the last decade, I've learnt when to put Andi in a cage, and when to let them out. At the right time, Andi is a phenomenal motivator and source of courage. At the wrong time, Andi is manipulative, abusive, and debilitating. In times of intense emotional fatigue, when all coping mechanisms are exhausted, Andi is a colossal raging monster. A crouched beast with piercing red eyes, clutching in bony talons my fragile resolve. Squeezing, talons all but piercing the protective sheath like a child taunts a swollen water balloon. One slight movement and the latex is pierced, the membrane violently tearing away. Resolve ruptured. A catastrophic, uncontrollable release of anything I ever thought I had contained.

Over the years, what brings out Andi's talons has evolved.

In my early memories, it was simply going to bed or being dropped off at school. It then became sleeping over at friends' houses, applying for casual jobs, or catching public transport. As my control of Andi grew stronger, it took getting out of my car to open the gate at the end of my very long driveway in the dark, or going to university, to reveal the talons. Falling pregnant, becoming a parent, and managing myself in a most challenging relationship strengthened my ability to keep Andi in a cage and be more strategic about letting them out when it was advantageous. It took major, somewhat traumatic events for Andi to become unhinged. The events of Good Friday evening in 2016 are a prime example.

2016

PROMISE - A letter to myself

In years to come I'm sure you'll question many of the parenting decisions you've made, as you have already. Remember what your uncle said to you: There isn't one single right decision. You just need to make sure that you choose one of the right ones.

I'm writing this letter to assure you that the decision you have just made is unequivocally one of the right ones for Sebastian. He is a sensitive, vulnerable child for whom you are responsible. It is your job to keep him safe, to help him to be happy, and to guide him in the right direction of becoming a well-adjusted, positive contributor to society. The decision that he will not have contact with his father is the right one. If there comes a time when Sebastian requests to have contact, ask yourself, are you confident Sebastian will be safe, both physically and psychologically, while in his care? If you cannot say that you are, then the time has not come for contact to be made.

I need you to remember:

The horrific dread that you felt when you received that text from Sebastian on Good Friday night in 2016. *Help me. Dad's drunk. I'm scared. Come to the unit. Now.*

The terror in his crying and hysterical voice in the subsequent phone calls where he pleaded *Hurry up and save me from Dad. Hurry up.*

The feeling of waiting for hours for police to arrive in the car park at the bottom of that city riverside apartment, imagining the most heinous scenarios possibly unfolding in the unit above.

The serious contemplation that Sebastian could have been violently hurt, or worse, and that you were powerless to stop it.

His father's scathing words and violent tone when he called you after the police had completed their welfare check, and again when you entered the unit number to collect Sebastian.

The viciousness in his screaming voice as you heard him

through the intercom yelling at Sebastian *You're never seeing me again. You're never coming back here... Ever!*

That his girlfriend is not a suitable caregiver. She must think his behaviour is acceptable and an appropriate way for a father to treat his son. She believes that he, the adult, is the one who is upset and needs love and compassion and protection in moments like this. No. Again. Parenting is a responsibility, not a right.

Remember the day after when Sebastian was giving you a step-by-step recount of the events of the previous night. The obscene language thrown at him in a fit of anger, not to mention objects that were hurled at him as his father's temper raged.

Remember that your precious and vulnerable Sebastian feared enough for his own life that he called 000. And then called again.

Remember how his father did not have enough respect for his own son to find the humility to take responsibility for his actions; and instead told his family that police were called because you overreacted to unanswered phone calls and text messages, and not because Sebastian feared for his life as a result of his father's abuse.

Remember the episodes Sebastian had in the weeks after this traumatic event where he would cry uncontrollably, his body rigid, his skin red, sweating profusely. Biting himself as all coping mechanisms had been exhausted. Remember Sebastian asking questions, 'Do you know what it's like to hate your own dad?' And you needing to be the one to explain that you don't know what that's like because no one should know what that's like.

Remember the extreme impact that Friday night had on you as you experienced the powerlessness to protect your child from harm.

Remember the indescribable guilt you felt when the first thing Sebastian said to you was *'What took you so long?'* He wasn't to know you'd been there, waiting, for hours. The constant fear that he would turn up at your house and take Sebastian or attempt to collect him from school without your knowing. The fear that your house keys were in his house. An uncaged and unhinged Andi planting vivid nightmares in your mind that wake you reacting as if he had organised a home invasion.

Remember the instant terror the first time you saw his name appear on your phone as he sent you a text message: Pounding heart, dripping sweat, literal trembling with fear of the unknown.

Remember the relief when the text was asking what I'm doing about Sebastian's school bag, and the further respite when that was sorted out by your brother-in-law.

Remember, that if this is how it is affecting you, it is exponentially worse for Sebastian.

Above all, remember that you are the adult. Remember, that when your empathy begins to creep back in, put it aside and find your authority. It is your responsibility to ensure your children are safe, even if that is from their other parent. Your line has been crossed. Do not give him the opportunity to push further past it and further damage this precious little boy you love so much.

You are doing the right thing. This is the right decision. Children have rights, parents have responsibilities. Sebastian has a right to be safe, and it is your responsibility to ensure it.

Remember.

2017-2019

AMBIVALENCE

Being Sebastian's parent has always been a significant challenge. Parenting, in whatever constitutes the ideal scenario, is challenging. You're dealing with people, rapidly growing people, complex relationships, and shared responsibility. This, compounded by falling pregnant at 18, to someone you're not in love with, someone whose values, perceptions, and ethical standards are starkly misaligned with your own; someone who has a warped sense of right and wrong, rights and responsibilities, of pride and shame, has made parenting Sebastian especially difficult. Despite Sebastian's brilliance, he is inattentive, impulsive, and disorganised. He's anxious, was often sick as a baby and young child, and has never slept well. Managing this highly complex situation, holding the responsibility of parenting as my highest priority, while also working to progress myself, is difficult. To say the least.

I am acutely aware that to say parenting an adolescent is a challenge is quite the understatement. Despite the absence of his father simplifying much of the adolescent parenting journey, the years between 11 and 16 are tough. These are also the years where the complexities associated with a blended family and parenting alongside a stepparent come to the fore.

Throughout the teenage years my increasing frustrations are met with persistent nagging. The homework not done, the assignments not submitted, the wet towels on the bathroom or bedroom floor, the dishes left around the house, the sneaky borrowed phone with the sneaky social media account, the girls invited over for the day when no one was home, the deceit, the arguing, and the back chatting. The feelings of not belonging to the family were likely regular, despite Sebastian only voicing them sporadically and only when in distress. Not yet an adult, but much older than the three siblings, creates a sense of isolation that none of us know how to combat. The importance of a sense of belonging during identity formation is not lost on me, but the knowledge of how to build it in this scenario is sadly trial and error.

Sometimes my emotional response to parenting is ambivalent. I am raising four children, from toddlers to teen, while in passionate pursuit of career progression and nurturing a love-filled marriage. In this multi-faceted life, priorities often seem in competition. The frequency of simultaneous and contradictory emotional responses to the life I'm leading is highly complex and often overwhelming. It's a lot.

I like a life that is busy and full. I enjoy operating at

capacity and constantly stretching and growing my capability. Remembering to leave room for the unexpected is not something I've been very good at. Knowing when to just admire your cake, and when to eat it too. Knowing when it's okay to eat in a civilised manner and when it's okay to bite off what looks like more than you can chew but committing to chewing like hell. The cup of life should be full. I enjoy a high surface tension, where life bulges above the rim. However, when you're thrown an extra and unexpected drop, life overflows.

2020

MY SHREDDED HEART – Shared with My Inner Circle

I'm sorry that there's absolutely nothing you can do to make me feel better or to help me. That's probably my biggest struggle. I am genuinely powerless. God grant me the serenity, right? If stress makes you skinny, then I may well start to fade away. There's got to be a silver lining. Surely it can be that I shed a few kilos.

I would literally need hours to tell you the whole story. You'll have questions. I'm unsure of my current ability to answer them.

Firstly, sorry for not being relaxed when we hung out recently. Potentially even a bit snappy. I was already not coping the best with the demands of this new job, how magnified that has been through Covid, as well as the usual demands of parenting four children across all the phases of development. If only I knew what was coming.

Tuesday afternoon I receive this text from Sebastian:

> *I'm not coming home tonight. I have somewhere safe to stay and will still be going to school. I don't want you to message me.*

I threaten to call the police to get him to have a very brief phone conversation where I find out he is staying at his grandmother's. Long story short he's been there ever since. She has no boundaries and is openly telling me she's not encouraging him to talk to me.

> *I don't want to push him. He could turn to drugs or suicide.*

I have very little insight into why he's doing this. It seems like very normal teenage emotions as a result of not enjoying your home/family. 'Normal' teenagers don't have a house to just slop around in after running away from home where they get thrown money and freedom. She has literally given him $50 a day for three days.

He turns 16 next Friday. I'm sure he thinks he's an adult, despite making some horrifically childish decisions.

I have no hope anymore that he is coming home. Genuinely. I'm not being dramatic. My hope is that he has a conversation with me at some stage. He barely engages in text messages and hangs up on me when I call.

Nothing in my entire life has ever been as exhausting or as isolating as the decisions and actions I have had to take in the raising of this child. I am so tired.

...

Tonight will be his eighth night away. He has not once voluntarily let me know where he is staying. His grandmother told me she would contact me daily to let me know he was there; I haven't heard from her since Monday. I spoke to her on Saturday. She is well-intentioned but has no idea. She was an average parent to Sebastian's father twenty years ago when teenage life was significantly less complex, so she has absolutely no hope with Sebastian. He is literally up all night most nights. She is allowing him to play on her fears, she is openly enabling him in an attempt to earn trust and not push him away.

School is powerless. They are doing all they can. One man, in particular, is managing the intricate balance of supporting Sebastian and supporting me like an absolute champion. Empathising with me, listening to me, and keeping me updated with his attendance and checking on him daily. If they would allow it, Sebastian would have already started the process of becoming an independent student. They really can't make him do anything. Just like the police. Unfortunately, there's no law against being a dick or disrespecting your mother. Damn that free will I spent years instilling in him.

Today Sebastian has communicated with me via text more than before and is being a lot less rude. That's something. I suspect this is because he wants things from our house. He asked if he could come home and get things from his room during the day when no one was there. I said no. He refuses to communicate any of his future intentions around when or if he ever intends on coming home or where he plans to live long-term. He stipulates that I am not to contact him at all, indefinitely, until he's ready. It is the most ludicrous power play that I am largely refusing to engage with. He has communicated that *it would be easiest* if I keep paying his phone bill. He understands he is welcome home any time and that I love him.

...

He thinks he's behaving like an adult. He is not. Not remotely. Not in any way. It's infuriating having to deal with his behaviour and not being able to respond the way I want. Continuing to do what I think is right and best, rather than what I want, is exhausting. Part of me really wants to treat him how I might treat any other adult. I even called his father today – that's how desperate I am. Not surprising, he didn't answer. I left a voice mail and don't expect him to return the call. I have learnt that Sebastian has been texting his father for a couple of weeks now, and that he is aware that Sebastian is

AGAPE

at his grandmother's. I don't know how I feel about it. I'm not sure what I should feel about it. All the feelings. All the things. It's a lot.

I am okay. In this moment right now. You never can tell what the next moment will bring. I don't have a choice but to cope. So, I am coping. Coping is very subjective. Much like being okay. Sometimes I completely and utterly fall apart, am void of emotional resources, and all my body wants to do is vomit. Sometimes I am insanely angry - with Sebastian, with his grandmother, with the world. And my deep-seated hatred for his father resurfaces. Sometimes when we're at the dinner table as a family I am overwhelmed with sadness. So often I habitually put six plates out as I set the table, and suddenly realise I only need five. The realisation that Sebastian is not there. He's missing. Our family is incomplete. I leave to get myself together. Again, I'm wondering if my decisions are best. Should I protect the little three from my emotion? Should I demonstrate vulnerability? I'm at a loss knowing how to communicate what I'm feeling and why. So, I shield them. I have never had a single grey hair in my life, and overnight they have appeared and are everywhere, and I am even angry about that.

Silver lining? Other than that now framing my face. The house is incredibly clean and tidy; Sebastian obviously made the most mess. Without question, I have not been putting more effort into keeping the house. I basically come home and crack a beer or pour myself a wine. Telling myself I deserve it. Why not? Alcohol consumption is an appropriate and effective coping mechanism. Right? I also have less washing to do. Who knows, maybe this time I'll be one of the lucky ones whose stress leads to weight loss! I hear humour is also an effective coping mechanism.

I don't care who you tell. But I really don't want to hear from people, and I don't want to hear their opinions. I would rather you only tell people who will not judge Sebastian's character, or qualify his worth, based on this shitty behaviour. His conduct is nonsensical. I cannot find a reasonable explanation for it. I'm aware this doesn't mean there isn't one. He's not a horrible person and I'm reasonably confident I could die tomorrow and he'd still grow into a decent man. I just don't know when. The last thing I want is a return or reunion to be more uncomfortable than necessary. My Aunty wasn't to know, but I already had to field a conversation from her on Sunday about using Covid as a time to reflect and reconsider how you live your life. People with my job and my home situation have definitely not been provided an opportunity for additional downtime for reflection during Covid. It's constant problem solving and preparing for possible future scenarios. Reflecting on my life choices might have me revisit my chosen career or the decision to have children. Not particularly realistic, helpful or favourable reflection.

Talking can be quite the emotional rollercoaster but it's important to me that you're across what's happening. I'm only committed to keeping you guys up to date. I can't manage to communicate the situation regularly to more people than that. Never wonder if it's okay for you to call or text or ask questions. You guys are different. You're my people. I love you all.

2020

MY SHREDDED HEART – A Letter Never Sent

Just your age plus two when I learnt you were being woven in my womb and was instantly isolated in overwhelming responsibility. While in the beginning, your dad may have been beside me in body, he in no way shared the responsibility. No one did. I carried that alone.

In that moment, you – your health, your happiness, and your future – became my highest priority. Every decision carefully considered and made with your wellbeing at the fore, regardless of how difficult that was, or what sacrifices needed to be made. Including learning who I was.

For all parents, the expectations of society at large, as well as those in your innermost circle, are often the loudest voices. I committed myself to ensuring that your needs drowned that out, that your needs were the loudest voice in my mind. I let that voice command me. As you grew older, I delicately balanced the necessity of listening to your actual voice with the weight of parental responsibility.

And for what?

I am exhausted. Completely and utterly shattered. An empty shell with not much more to offer. You are, undeniably, the one thing I have poured every ounce of my being into – every moment and every single decision from conception. And I did it alone. The unfathomable self-control and relentless, painstaking consideration I put into managing your father to ensure best outcomes for you. The lawyers, the psychologists, the reduced family assistance as a result of forfeiting my rights to child support, the knowledge that I was forgoing thousands, tens of thousands of dollars of child support each year, because it would avoid conflict and decrease the likelihood of harm to you. The watching you not only be continuously let down but abused by your father, year after year after year, because child protection's threshold is unacceptably high and what they deem to be acceptable is vastly different to the standard I hold people to, especially with regards to the treatment of you, my child.

After 16 years, to have you pick all of that up, throw it in my face, run away, and crawl into the lap of the family who made your life a living hell a whole fucking lot of the time, has been a very, very, jagged pill to swallow.

It took a few weeks to get it down. But I did. I also

swallowed my pride. I know this is not something you are doing to me. It is something you must do for you. I have given you what you asked for – space, freedom. I have made sure that you know you are loved and missed, and that I am here. I was, and continue to be, scared of where your life could go under their influence in what are likely the most crucial years of identity development. My comforting thought has been that when I look back on my carefully considered parenting decisions I don't wish I did anything differently. I know, unequivocally, that every decision I made, I made for you, to provide you with the best. My comfort is in knowing that your character is founded in strength and integrity.

Today, my fears were realised. Your judgement was off. You did a stupid thing and needed genuine unconditional love. The opportunity for me to be there and pick up the pieces was stripped from me. The opportunity to have me, your mum, there to comfort you and to remind you that we make mistakes, and let you know that together we will make things better, was taken away from you. How dare they.

I am livid. Seething. With them. All of them. Hate is a blistering word, but it may just be appropriate here. They continue, as they have done for the almost twenty years I have known them, to make the most selfish decisions. They hide behind a mask of putting you first, when to them you're a trophy. They welcomed you in under the guise of saving you, out of fear that you would turn to drugs or suicide. And look where we are now. Forgiveness is something I will strive for –

but not for their benefit. For mine. I do not deserve to harbour such a black place in my heart, and they do not deserve to occupy any part of me.

Teenagers are like toddlers. They have a deep need for both greater independence and tender loving care. The speed of growth in your adolescent brain means you're frequently confused and often frustrated. Not only do you feel misunderstood, but you also don't understand yourself. You are in a critical period that will impact the rest of your life. You are one of the most intelligent people I know, but because you're a teenager, your decision-making is overly influenced by your untamed emotions. You have developed an enormous skill set, but you're not the best at putting it into practice yet. I will continue to remind myself that your actions are not a personal attack on me. Teenagers often misread adults, and adults often misread teenagers. I am here. Ready and waiting to listen for understanding.

Even if from a distance. Even if in silence. Know that I am here. I am here to listen. I am here to learn. I am here to be what you need.

If calling on me will never be an option for you, please remember: the only real mistake is one you don't learn from. Your intellect is strong, but your character is stronger. Most importantly, remember that even when you feel most alone, I am with you.

CLARET SAGE

I believe in you. I miss you. I love you.

Mum.

2020

MY SHREDDED HEART –
Invaluable Unfiltered Friendship

These six months have been full of learning. I learnt that I am empathetic and forgiving, compromising and flexible, and generally assume others are doing their best. I also learnt that I will only be those things for so long, and it doesn't matter who you are, I know my worth and will not be taken advantage of. Once again, I have a line. In the beginning it might be blurry, but every so often, the closer people get to it, it comes into sharp focus, and compromise ceases.

Again, the opinions of others through this time have been difficult to hear. Especially from those closest to me. Logically, I assume others are doing their best, and doing what they think is right. But it feels like judgement. What I need is empathy, reassurance, and support.

While I'm sure it isn't as calculated or intentional as it feels, Sebastian drip feeds tiny diamonds of hope, and every single time follows it up with a demand for money or possessions, without ever communicating the why or the vision for the near or distant future. I give, and I give, and I give. And get nothing. I feel disrespected. Taken advantage of. I feel used and devalued. One last request has me give Sebastian all I have left. I transfer every dollar of savings that I had saved for him into his bank account, and I pack up his entire bedroom into two large boxes and leave them on the driveway for collection. I tell him, clearly and directly, I will continue to pay his phone bill and his school fees for now, but be sure to know, in no uncertain terms, that without any effort from him to rebuild a quality and mutually respectful relationship, I was done giving.

Many people think this is callous. Many people tell me 'You simply can't do that'. Many people feel the need to remind me that a mother's love is unconditional. Sometimes I challenge. Sometimes it's not worth the energy to find the words. But ultimately, while my love as a mother might be unconditional, my respect is not. My respect is conditional. My commitment to show my children – all four of them – that you are responsible for your own happiness, and that you have the right to be treated with respect. By all people. That no one has the right to treat you with contempt, no matter who they are. On this, I am uncompromising.

One friend, Stephanie, is a steadfast supporter through

this time. Her disbelief matches mine and she is impressed by my rationality. It's hard to put into words what exactly she does for me, but she did say, 'What hope do other parents have? You parented Sebastian in a consistent manner, with clear, reasonable, and immovable boundaries, with respect and discussion, and yet he has still defiantly rebelled.' This is so incredibly validating. It validates the lack of guilt I feel, the faith I have in my parenting style and my commitment to it, and the acknowledgement that if I had known this was going to happen, I still would not have done anything differently. Validation that the likelihood of long-term positive outcomes is still high. Layla, again, has come to my rescue. I'm not sure I believe in God, and I'm not sure it even matters, but I am sure that there is more than luck and coincidence to have these two women carrying me through these times. Their unwavering support, their gentle challenge, and their acceptance of me. And perhaps more importantly, their acceptance of Sebastian.

Stephanie and Layla are the two people I talk to without filter, without careful selection of words. I can be totally and completely vulnerable. Share my biggest challenges, my greatest fears, and the nuance of the stress that permeates my home and my relationship through this time. This is invaluable.

INFINITE

ARLO

And then there's Arlo. It hurts Arlo when I express how alone I feel. How isolating I have found the parenting of Sebastian, and that the grief of this particular experience has intensified that feeling significantly. I was broken. On one occasion I felt but a shell of a human, that I had nothing left to give. To anyone. Completely disconnected. And Arlo was afraid. I could see it in his eyes. And yet in that moment I had not an ounce of empathy. I was empty. But he held me. And he listened. And he reassured. He put aside his own feelings – whatever they were – and physically and metaphorically held me together until I was strong enough to keep going.

This must have taken extreme courage. This selfless love. Arlo has been there, every step of the way, for the past 14 years. Been there for me and been there for Sebastian. Working hard, as we both were, not to be pulled into the dramatic triangle of victim, rescuer, persecutor, as can so easily happen in the parent, child, stepparent dynamic. Working hard alongside me to recognise when either of us had regressed into one of these roles and committing to be conscious and intentional in all interactions. Sebastian does not remember a time in his life before Arlo, but the relationship has been fickle and somewhat arduous. There have been moments of brilliance, but for the three of us, it's been hard work. I'm sure I'm not the only one to feel the isolation, the enervation. I have struggled to communicate the emotion of isolation accurately over the years, because I feel incredibly loved and supported by an enormous network of people. But oh, so incredibly alone, in the responsibility of parenting Sebastian and managing all the relationships and competing priorities that encompass that responsibility. I'm sure Arlo and Sebastian are just as lonely.

Arlo is incredible. From the first time he visited my house with Sebastian at home, when I watched him genuinely interested in building an authentic relationship; to the first time he had Sebastian in his care without me, where he bathed him, played with him, and fed him dinner, all before I arrived home from my summer holiday job; to being the parent who did all the school drop-offs and pickups when he was at home with Michael and studying; to giving all of himself and never taking a back foot in this step-parenting gig. It used to piss me off when people would tell me Arlo had sacrificed so much to be there for me and Sebastian, and herald him a hero. What they meant to say was that they would never have considered entering a relationship with someone with a two-year-old. Especially when they were only 23. This has never been something I've been especially grateful for. No one forced his hand.

CLARET SAGE

He made an active and informed decision. What I am grateful for is the deliberate consideration Arlo gave such a heavy decision. The decision to continue a relationship with me once falling in love became a reality. Deciding to move to the more significant, committed stage of a romantic relationship was more loaded in this situation, and Arlo recognised that. He respected it. He valued the emotional wellbeing of the two-year-old. He knew that Sebastian deserved that consideration. And I know that Arlo felt the weight of it. I am grateful he recognised the importance of that decision and gave it the consideration it deserved.

I don't believe in soul mates. I don't believe that in all the billions of people in this world, there is only one true love for me. I don't believe that I need to be in love to be complete. I don't believe in any level of certainty when it comes to knowing you're going to spend the rest of your life with someone. I am certain that Arlo is my love. Because I chose him. And he chose me. And my love, without question, has conditions. I believe everyone's romantic love should have conditions. And Arlo consistently meets those conditions. Our love is beautiful, and raw, and messy, and passionate, and honest, and so completely human, imperfect, and fragile. We are not the people we were all those years ago when he invited me to that party in his seedy share house. And our love is not the love that first sparked late that evening. It's grown and matured and is equally as beautiful, and so much more valuable. The best relationship advice I have ever been given was written by my mother in our wedding card. *Treat your relationship with the fragility it deserves.* Love is a fragile thing, even the most genuine love. You need to nurture it. You remain hope-filled that this love is eternal. But never, ever, make the mistake of assuming that is guaranteed. When you remain conscious of this, you remain passionately in love and grateful for the opportunity. And it's easier to do when you have yourself an Arlo.

2020

THE ANGELS CAME TO PLAY

It's a late November afternoon and I receive a call from Sebastian's school. He's not in a good way. He has nowhere to go. He can't go to his father's. He can't go to his grandmother's. I have no idea why. No context at all. I don't need it. I get in my car, leave work, and immediately drive to collect Sebastian from school. I am grateful for the long drive, as there is much to consider. One thing I know for sure. He cannot come to our family home this evening. He does not get to live the last six months the way he did, treat me and our family the way he did, and just walk right back in to be welcomed with open arms. He is returning, ultimately, because he is out of options. He has lived the disturbing experience of immersion in his father's family. An experience that I know all too well and remember as though it was yesterday. He found his line, but he still can't see mine. He can't see that he leaped over mine and is so far past it that he can barely see it when he turns to look back. I am hope filled. But I am realistic, and

I know myself. And I know that if there is a repeat of the last six months, that if he chooses to leave without warning and cease communication, if he continues to take without giving, if he continues to abuse the relationship further and not work to restore it, there will be no return. And I need to make sure that's not going to happen. I need him to know, without a shadow of a doubt, where my line is. My love is unconditional. But my like, my understanding, my respect, my forgiveness - they most certainly have conditions.

I collect Sebastian from school and drive him to my parents' house. It's a very quiet drive. My words are few – I'm glad you called. I'm glad you're coming home. I've missed you. His words fewer still. Happiness and sadness are entangles in my chest in equal measure. I have no insight into the emotions that may be twisted in his.

In the scheme of things, it was a short transition home. He spent a total of two weeks living at my parents, with a gradual transition to the family home that included many purposeful conversations with Sebastian, Arlo and me. There has been acceptance, expressions of hurt, communication of intent or lack of it, and an agreement to move forward with mutual respect and a commitment to seeking understanding.

The Christmas break and the following year are interesting and plagued with frustration, misunderstanding, a severe misalignment between intent and impact, and trust built up and broken down. Arlo and I take a risk and go away for the weekend with Michael, Jimmy, and Thomas in toe, leaving Sebastian at home. He is 17. It is the most catastrophic severing of the trust that had been rebuilt over the past six months. We arrive home to smashed glass on the street at our driveway. Interesting. I know he had a friend over on one of the nights. I move my car from the garage to create room to unpack from camping. When I turn on the ignition, I am blown away by both the air conditioning and deafening obnoxious music. Someone has driven my car. Deep breaths. I walk into the house and out the back door – remnants of more smashed glass, and evidence of cigarettes. Heart racing. So. Many. Deep. Breaths. And I realise just how fragile trust is. Just how quickly it can be broken after so much work to rebuild.

2021 is a year, much like each of those in the past, where I am constantly reminding myself that I am the only thing I can control. I am the only thing I can change. My thoughts, my attitudes, my perceptions, my words, and my actions. They are all I have in my power. It is a year of learning that I am a happier, calmer, more productive person when I learn to accept and let go. This learning, however, made the definition of where my line is significantly more difficult.

2021

GRADUATION

Here we are. 13 years of schooling done.

From the day the privilege and challenge of being your mum was gifted to me it has been one gloriously wild ride, every memory alive and vivid.

It's been heart-wrenching and heart-warming. I have smiled infinite smiles, cried countless tears, laughed uncontrollably, and (more frequently than I'd like to admit) spoken through gritted teeth. The adventure has been epic to say the least.

Your incredible resourcefulness, your ability to find joy in the darkest of times, and your commitment to being yourself and forging your own path in a world that so often tries to box us in to fit a certain mould are but a few of the things I admire most in you.

Congratulations on writing one hell of an historical

narrative over the past 17 or so years. Go set the world on fire (figuratively speaking!).

I am because we are.

Thank you.

I love you.

2022

RELIEF AND ANGUISH 2.0

I am because we are. While this parenting journey has been a monumental challenge, I am a better person because of it. I look back on the teenager who was yet to learn how to manage Andi. The teenager who second-guessed herself all the time, who left university the first time around because navigating the tiniest campus was overwhelming, who would call in sick to work because she couldn't lock Andi's cage, who put up with gaslighting, coercive control and aggressive behaviour from her boyfriend, the father of her baby, because doing what was *right* was more important than acknowledging her own worth. The experience of raising Sebastian challenged me to be better. I wasn't strong enough to choose to be better. To choose to be better for me. Sebastian was my reason. A reason to be the ultimate role model. A reason to be strong. A reason to be my best self. A reason to belong wherever I am and to never betray myself.

That strength has been tested. Repeatedly. And this year -

despite formal schooling being over, despite the commitment to never speaking to or interacting with his father ever again - was not going to be any different.

...

As I reflect on my parenting journey, which today is 18 years long, I am overwhelmed with an array of emotions I struggle to name.

Today we celebrate the man, and the journey of raising him: a thrilling, unpredictable, surreal, agonising, heart-warming, perplexing, yet incredibly rewarding ride. While surrounded and supported by the most wonderful people imaginable, this journey has been more isolating than anything I've experienced. And I was not prepared for that. I've learnt that there is no such thing as insurmountable challenge, and that I wouldn't have achieved the things I have if I wasn't thrust into the challenge and privilege of this journey, just barely into adulthood myself. The most valuable lesson has been true acknowledgment that I cannot control anything outside of myself, and learning to see this as a comfort rather than a source of angst.

Happy Birthday Sebastian. You're a dead set legend. Your ocean eyes, cheeky smirk, and preference for being awake all night are a few things that have remained since infancy. You have an uncanny radical trust in the world that everything will work out as it should. You possess the frustrating yet admirable skill of letting things go and moving on without discussion, and you undoubtedly have a knack for landing on your feet in the most unlikely circumstances. Sebastian, we know you'll not only 'sort it out' but achieve greatness. And I expect you to do so in the least conventional way. Thank you for gifting me motherhood.

To those at the heart of my expansive village, my parents, my sisters and their husbands: thank you for riding the waves alongside me, for knowing when to support me and when to challenge me. And for reliably doing the same for Sebastian.

It's no secret this has been a tumultuous ride at times, and while I can't practically thank each individual in the village, there are a few key players who I must. I'm not sure where I'd be if you'd not literally held me together or rebuilt me when the pieces fell apart.

Layla, for your enduring lack of judgement, your sound advice, and for holding me together and building me up in the very beginning when I needed it most.

Rebekah, for giving me the courage to make one of my most difficult life decisions, and for holding me together and lifting me up in the aftermath.

Emily and Joey, for journeying with me every step of the way, whether near or far, for the compassion, the understanding, and the insight.

Aiobhe, for listening and empathising when I thought love might kill me and I just needed to put one foot in front of the other.

Stephanie, for so much, but mostly for validating my thoughts and emotions, for nothing being off limits, and for making me feel understood.

And of course, Arlo. Words cannot adequately express my gratitude. Thank you for your authenticity and for enjoying reality rather than striving for fantasy. For seeing rough patches as progression, and for acknowledging that everything takes a really (really) long time. Thank you for not taking it personally when I express feelings of isolation. Thank you for rising to the challenge alongside me and journeying the extraordinary road that it's been. We worked hard at the work worth doing, and the world will reap the benefits. We make a formidable team.

...

Sebastian's plan during his first year out of school is to enjoy not having to live by anyone else's rules, not having to meet anyone else's expectations, to sleep as much as he wants and to stay awake as long as he wants. Six months in and he's kicking his goal out of the park. He seems happy. But it's very hard to tell. I am struggling. Struggling, again, to accept what I perceive to be a lack of progress, and drive. Struggling to admire his ability to know what he wants, to be completely present. He has good friends. Mostly. He has relationships I

AGAPE

find so incredibly interesting. And by that, I mean confusing. He has a job. One he loves. His social game is his strength, and he's using it to his advantage by working in hospitality. His patrons love him. He feels a sense of achievement. His six months out of our home delayed him obtaining his learner license for a whole list of reasons. He has had his learner's for six months now but is not interested in clocking up the hours with me as the supervising driver. When I accompany him driving, the rolling eyes are frequent and the *I know everything* attitude is rife.

While there is a sense of relief that school is over, the frustration is regularly high. There is still a lingering sense of disregard for me and Arlo. A lack of remorse for what we've been put through, and an absence of gratitude for how we've responded. I continue to work on acceptance rather than searching for solutions, especially when I am likely the only one who sees things as a problem. I continue to acknowledge that Sebastian does not need my approval for how he lives his life. Sometimes it's okay to acknowledge that you don't understand, you're never going to understand, and accept that things will unfold as they should. This is a challenge like no other.

...

Sebastian is calling. I am in a shopping centre car park. He tells me that a few days ago he was arrested and charged with a string of driving related offenses. But it's fine. His dad is sorting it out.

Hold that thought.

If you can.

Remind yourself to breathe.

Mentally implode.

You've got to be fucking kidding me!

Deep, deep breath.

And again.

And only then was I somewhat prepared to speak out loud.

I empathise. Listen. Express disappointment and concern.

I calmly explain…

> *I need you to know, that I have experience with this sort of thing with all the young people I have supported at work who've gloriously fucked up just like you have. Your dad is the worst person you could have to sort this out for you. He is your worst character reference and your best reason for explaining your behaviour. I suggest it would*

AGAPE

be wise to let me help you to ensure the best possible outcome. The potential ramifications of this are staggering.

He listens. I think he's feeling pretty shit about himself. And while I don't enjoy that he feels that way, there is comfort in knowing there is some level of shame. Some level of something. It's not apathy. He messages me later. Short and simple. But appreciated. *Thank you for the way you reacted.* It's early August. Court is scheduled for mid-September.

I expected to see remorse through an outward display of commitment to self-improvement. Why do I continue to be so naïve? Why do I continue to assume and expect the best? How am I not learning? I have always thought I was an optimistic realist. Aunty Kate once told me I wasn't. During one after dinner conversation at my parents' place, with a smug little smile on her face, she firmly put me in my place, informing me that I was most definitely an idealist under the illusion that I was a realist. That was about fifteen years ago. I am just beginning to think she was right.

I arrange a lawyer, enrolment in an online traffic rehabilitation course, and schedule time away from work to accompany him on the day. The six weeks between the offense and the court date are painful in more ways than one. I am in emotional and financial debt, only one of which I expect him to repay. Surely that's not idealistic?

Court is a new experience. For both of us. Dispassionate.

Neither positive nor negative. It just... is. The response is fair. An appropriate inconvenience to encourage reflection and learning. Sebastian thanks me, sincerely. And I appreciate it.

The drive home is interesting. He clearly feels relief. But there is a frustrating air of nonchalance with regard to next steps. I work hard not to voice my concern and frustration. With the possibility that he could have been going to jail, especially if he didn't adhere to subsequent stipulations, nonchalance is not what I was expecting. But again, I breathe. Slow. And Deep.

I do wonder sometimes when this will result in hyperventilation.

2022

THE STOLEN UNDIES

I'll let your mind wander and conjure up some elaborate story behind the chapter title. But it leads to an unpleasant text exchange with feelings of significant violation of personal boundaries and disrespect on one side, and intense injustice on the other. Seemingly insignificant, it is the first *real* conflict between Arlo and Sebastian as adult peers rather than parent and child.

I am over it. Done. Sick of figuring out which role I need to play in this drama. Whose need I should work to meet. Choosing the side of morality, compassion, and understanding, and not this side or that, repeatedly disappoints everyone. I am checking out. I let them both know I am very sad about the interaction and the situation. I let them know I do and have always worked hard to understand each side, and that I am full of empathy for each of them. I tell each of them that I'm done allowing their relationship with each other to impact my relationship with each of them. It's not the first time I've said this, but it was the first time I really meant it. They are to leave me out of it.

Interestingly, each of them asks me what they should do, independently of each other. After checking whether this is genuine, I tell them what I think. And I tell them both the same thing. First, reflect. What part of this is your responsibility? What could you have done differently? Done better? How do you think your words and actions impacted the other? Own it. Acknowledge it. And apologise for it. Start there. Consider that intention and impact are misaligned. Go so far as to assume they are well intentioned and unaware of their significant negative impact. Communicate the impact they had on you and do so without contempt. Then, you listen. Genuinely. Listen with the goal of true and deep understanding. Then, you will be able to work towards a common understanding and mutual respect.

They listened. And then… they asked me to be with them when they had the conversation.

So here I am. Involved. Despite my best efforts and genuine commitment not to be. But it is at their request. Which took days.

I don't know what this says about me, but it was awesome. I felt like everything I had been hoping and dreaming of was coming to fruition. To say I am proud might be patronising, but I can't find a more appropriate word. Like all conversations of this nature, it was uncomfortable, but the outcome was positive. Such a relief for me that the first adult conflict was resolved in an adult way.

2023

LIFE AND LEARNING

In this moment, I am content. I am careful not to be complacent. I know there will undoubtedly be more challenge. This beautifully arduous parenting journey that is raising Sebastian is far from complete. But for now, I'm all of the positive emotions. And I'm reflective. Through parenting Sebastian I have spent a lot of time reflecting in action, searching for a new perspective, and adjusting my views on things to affect positive change. I now have the space to reflect on action. To rise above the daily grind, the consuming nature of parental responsibility, and look back on the experience. Critique my parenting approach and its underpinning philosophy. There is so much to consider.

I am fiercely passionate about equality. A staunch feminist committed not only to empowering and supporting young women but to shaping a future where all obstacles to gender equality are removed. I have never mourned not having a daughter of my own. With each pregnancy, I genuinely did not have a preference for the baby's sex, and I never found out their sex before the day of their birth. Others struggled with this concept, some refusing to believe this perspective was possible, and simply thought I was hiding my shame of wishing my boy was a girl. Questions such as, 'what would you choose if you could choose? Or if you had to choose?' To which my response was that I simply wouldn't. If I had the opportunity, I would most definitely not want any part in choosing things such as sex, appearance, or aptitudes. This goes against my moral and ethical code. Perhaps that's why I've never had a preference.

When imagining the world I have been a part of shaping, I'm presented with an immense opportunity to raise boys to be adults in an equal world. To raise men who fight the good fight, working in grassroots activism to redefine masculinity, even if only by lived example in their daily lives. Men with a sound moral and ethical code, who are committed to listening to silenced voices and working towards a discrimination-free society where people seek first to understand.

There are times when I wonder what it would have been like to have that intimate influence on a strong woman. One who takes hold of her place in the world with authority, not assuming a passive position or conforming to oppressive societal conditions. This is usually when I'm confronted with a young girl who's not been shown that she can carve her own way in this world. That she doesn't need to follow in the footsteps in front of her. I am grateful that in these moments I am blessed with the opportunity to have some tiny influence on enlightening them. Likewise, I am grateful I have been afforded the privilege of bearing witness to many young girls growing into self-assured women. That I have the opportunity to walk alongside some inspiring mothers who've raised and are raising their daughters to be strong women who will forge their own path, unshackled by convention. There are times when I wonder what a daughter of mine would have been like. I have concluded that she would have been much like my sons.

The purpose of life is nothing more than experience. I guess that's why they say life is what you make it. It doesn't mean you get to determine life events or choose each twist and turn. But it does mean you get to determine how you experience it. Raising Sebastian has been, and continues to be, an experience. An adventure. A bold and complex undertaking that continues to be so incredibly rewarding.

There are moments where my confidence and belief in both myself and Sebastian wavers. There are shocking unexpected realisations and learnings that take time to process. But I am grateful and find solace in the fact that our relationship continues to mature and strengthen. My love as a parent remains steadfast and sincere. When at times it seems that it lay shattered on the floor I realise this is momentary. I wonder at times what my understanding of life would be had I not become a parent.

I will continue to live and allow my children to watch. My hope is that they learn. They will likely learn how they want to live, whether that is similar to what they've witnessed is up to them. I hope they learn how to master themselves, and to live peacefully within themselves, and within the environment they choose to embed themselves in. I hope that they love themselves unconditionally. That they learn how to forgive, both others and themselves. I want them to be compassionate, empathetic, and deliberate. And I want them to make good use of the question.

As a mother of four sons spanning twelve years, a successful professional, and in a most loving and respectful relationship, there has been much learning over the last almost forty years of life. But there has been one learning that trumps all else. One learning that has become my life's guiding principle that allows me to live a life without regret. Only growth, improvement, and learning. And ultimately, pride and satisfaction.

Everything is values-based. Everything. And at all times, actions and behaviours need to be aligned with personal values. There are many decisions that are right. You have to make sure you choose one of the right ones. Life is complex. And oftentimes, the right action, even one of the right actions, can be profoundly difficult to ascertain. The single, most important question I ask myself in these moments is: which decision can I live with if it's wrong? This philosophy is yet to let me down. I am yet to experience true regret.

So here I am. Content. Aware of what I can control and influence and I'm working with that. Proud of what I have achieved and how I've lived my life, and excited about what's to come. I'm learning not to take life too seriously. It's much more fun when you don't. I am grateful. So incredibly grateful for the hand I've been dealt and the one I've worked so hard to clasp. I am committed to achieving and being more every single day of my life. I believe with all my being that continuous improvement is the key to happiness and life satisfaction, and that is what I'm committed to.

The balancing act is ongoing. The work life, the home life, the healthy life, the active life, the learned life, the married life, the multi-age parenting life, the never-ending admin of life. There are times when I'm at capacity, times when I'm searching for more, and times when it all boils over and Andi emerges from the cage mauling me with their talons. And then I rinse and repeat.

I have been a mother for nineteen years. When Sebastian turns twenty next year, I will no longer be a mother of a teenager. I will have almost exactly eight months of reprieve before Michael turns 13. Once again, I will find myself guiding a reactive, highly emotional, oversized toddler who's prone to succumbing to pressure from peers and engaging in risky behaviour. Once again, I will find comfort in knowing that Arlo and I laid a solid moral foundation and that the character of our children is founded in strength and integrity. I will breathe deeply through tumultuous times. I will love harder than I've ever loved, and I will trust, sometimes blindly, that everything will unfold as it should. I will go placidly amid the noise and haste…

www.ingramcontent.com/pod-product-compliance
Lightning Source LLC
Chambersburg PA
CBHW052145070526
44585CB00017B/1976